Presentation Tactics

Strategies for Effective Sales Engagements

Objective 1: Preparation

Jeff Mildon

Printed in the United States of America

First Printing, 2024

ISBN: 9798879212372
Imprint: Independently published

To my wife Kristi and my kids Tyler, Kyra and Lilli
And to all my friends and family

Table of Contents

Introduction

I have been doing sales presentations and product demonstrations for the past 30 years for two medical software companies. I have created and performed over 10,000 presentations in my career. I have contributed about 300 million dollars in sales, resulting from my presentations. I have articles published in trade journals, and I speak at user conferences and national industry trade shows. I published my first book, Infotainment, Guide to Effective Sales Presentations in 2013.

I still remember two classes that I took back in high school that taught me lessons that I still employ in my professional life. The first was called College Preparatory Writing (Thanks Mrs. Bauer). The second was Debate (Thanks Mr. Nick). The first taught me to organize my thoughts and communicate in writing. The second taught me to organize my thoughts verbally, perform research, structure an argument, speak in front of people, question and cross-examine. I am thankful for the education that I received that taught and encouraged communication and always recommend people enhance their communication skills.

Presentations and public speaking skills are very useful in many aspects of work and life. Effective presentations and public speaking skills are important in business, sales, training, teaching, and generally entertaining an audience. Developing the confidence and capability to stand up in front of an audience and speak well, or to give a good presentation is also an extremely helpful competency for self-development. Like most things, delivering a successful presentation simply takes a little preparation and practice.

The formats and purposes of presentations can be very different, for example: oral (spoken), multimedia (using various media - visuals, audio, etc.), PowerPoint presentations, short impromptu presentations, long-planned presentations, educational or training sessions, lectures, and simply giving a talk on a subject to a group. Even a speech like a toast at a wedding or a eulogy at a funeral are types of presentations.

My first book explored presentations in one large volume. The follow-up books examine presentations in 3 parts. The first book (the one you are currently reading) talks about preparation. There will be activities before the presentation like planning, writing, development, equipment, discovery, etc. In my opinion, preparation is the biggest factor in a successful presentation.

The second book covers the techniques used during the presentation. Some of these presentation tips are prepared in advance but then used during the presentation.

Book number three talks about the activities after the presentation. We will discuss debriefing and evaluating feedback to help prepare for the next presentation.

Tips and tricks for presentations must be applied to a presenter's unique situation and style. Some guidelines can be universally applied and some need modification. When you learn new techniques, they must be internalized and made your own. A presenter can recite a memorized, canned presentation and follow all the right rules "by the book" and end up seeming not genuine to the audience. As an example, politicians that read speeches from a teleprompter, which somebody else wrote for them, always fall short of being genuine for me.

I think that providing information should be entertaining. Audience members are much more accepting of information and new ideas if presented in a positive fun manner.

Presenters must believe and care about what they are saying to be effective communicators. I am passionate about presenting and hopefully, I can instill some of that passion in you, the reader.

The first thing to do when you are going to give a presentation is to prepare. I am one of those people that would much rather be completely over-prepared. For me, setup is very important and is the one thing that can make or break your presentation. I will spend a significant amount of time about setup and preparation because that is where you spend most of your time as a presenter. In many instances, I have done several days of preparation for demonstrations that lasted less than an hour. The presentation flew by because I was prepared.

Preparation is the key to confidence, which is the key to you being relaxed. The most important rule for effective presentations is to prepare, which means you need to plan out your presentation, practice it, adjust, and practice again. Then you'll be in control and confident. Your audience will sense your confidence and respond accordingly. And dare we imagine, you might even start to enjoy yourself too. According to the Fred Pryor Organization, a significant provider of seminars and open presentation events, good preparation and rehearsal will reduce your nerves by 75%, increase the likelihood of avoiding errors 95%.

An Effective presentation is about entertaining as well as conveying information. People retain more if they are enjoying themselves and feeling relaxed. Whatever your subject and audience, try to find ways to make the content and delivery enjoyable. Even the most serious of occasions and the driest of subjects can be lifted to an enjoyable or even an amusing level, one way or another, with a little research, imagination, and humor. Enjoyment and humor are mostly in the preparation and confidence. You don't need to be a natural stand-up comedian to inject a little Infotainment into a presentation or talk. It's the content that enables it, which is very definitely within your control.

Chapter 1: Essential Gear

"Before anything else, preparation is the key to success."
Alexander Graham Bell

      A good presenter has a mental bag of tricks that they rely on. Your knowledge is the best tool that you can have. Along with your expertise and depending on your industry and products, there is certain equipment and gear essential for your presentation. Instead of relying on equipment to be provided at the location of the presentation, my tendency is to carry all my stuff. I like to be in control to lessen the likelihood of something going wrong or something essential not being available. When you practice your presentation, also practice with your gear. You will discover what works and what needs adjustment or replacement.

      My first piece of essential gear would be a device to provide a visual. This could be a PC, laptop, tablet, or other devices. I have done mostly live software product presentations, so I carry a tablet PC with the software that I am presenting, loaded on it. My vote will always go to carrying the fastest device possible with the most memory. It annoys me when a presenter makes excuses for a slow computer; although, I have made the same excuses myself. I also see some presenters connect to a remote computer or server instead of having the software loaded directly on their local machine.

      Your "device" might not even be a computer at all. I have seen very effective presenters use flip charts or whiteboards, even the old overhead projector. You can definitely go "no tech" with your presentation, and for those of you in the "no tech" category, many of the devices that we talk about next are unnecessary.

      There are several factors in deciding which piece of software and hardware to use:

1. Simple - ease of use is usually near or at the top of all lists.

2. Reliable - presenters expect the equipment to work.

3. Budget - each presenter and their company will differ as to the   amounts they can afford to spend on presentation equipment.

4. Flexible - if the equipment can be used for a variety of presentation needs, it will be used more for a lower cost, and I like equipment that can fulfill multiple roles.

5. Functional - the equipment should not interfere with the presentation. The equipment is not the show, so it should be supportive and not distracting. (Unless, of course, you are selling and demonstrating equipment)

Below is a checklist of different presentation equipment and multimedia technology, along with the pros and cons of each:

Writing Board (Includes Chalk and Blackboard or Dry Erase Board)

Pros:
Easy to use.
Inexpensive.
Easily annotate.
Easy to transport.

Cons:
It does not stay in front of the audience throughout the presentation, and it can be erased.
Must be able to write legibly.
Limited use of colors and graphics.

Flip Boards.

Stays in front of the audience if writing on paper is removed and mounted on poster board.
Inexpensive.
Easily annotate.
Easy to transport.

Cons:
Must be able to write legibly.
Limited use of colors and graphics.

Digital Flipchart.

Using a computer, a projector and the Digital Flipchart, the computer can be controlled at the whiteboard by the touch of your finger. This allows you to touch the screen to control the computer and to present and write on images, documents, etc. An example of a digital flipchart can be found at www.smarttech.com.

Pros:
Easily annotate on the whiteboard itself.
Reflects what is on the computer screen.
Controls computer from the whiteboard.
The screen is bright, so lights do not have to be dimmed.
Can print out screens to save.
Graphics can be used.

Cons:
You need to purchase or rent an LCD projector and digital flipchart.
Transportation - due to its size - can be difficult.
The cost is around $4000 for a digital flipchart.

Digital Whiteboard.

A digital whiteboard is a computerized note board. After writing on a computer "whiteboard" with a dry eraser the writing can be automatically printed onto an 8 ½ by 11-inch piece of paper.

Pros:
Easy to use.
Writing can be saved for later use.
Easy to annotate.

Cons:
Expensive - approximate cost is $5,000 to $10,000.
Transportation - due to its size - can be difficult.
Must be able to write legibly.
Limited use of colors and graphics.

Overhead Projector and Transparencies.

Pros:
Common and easy to use.
Generally easy to fix if a bulb burns out.
Easily annotate and draw on transparencies.
Can produce transparencies with laptop printer.
Generally, do not have to dim the lights.
Color or B/W.
Can enlarge to 8' by 10' or larger.
Graphics can be created beforehand.
Easy to transport.

Cons:
Projector noise can be distracting unless you have a newer model.
Images do not stay in front of an audience.

Blowups - graphics & documents:

Pros:
Stays in front of an audience throughout the presentation.
Can annotate if a clear sheet is placed over blowup.
The size of the poster board blowups is determined by the budget.
It can be inexpensive.
Relatively easy to transport.

Cons:

The cost can be expensive depending on who prepares it and the complexity of subject matter such as medical illustrations.

Visual Presenter

A video camera that projects objects, photographs, or paper to a monitor or to a screen using a projection device. Sometimes it is called a document camera.

Pros:

Easy to operate.
Can project objects, x-rays, paper, or photographs.
Can annotate on paper or photographs with special pens.
Saves the cost of enlarging photographs and documents.
Objects can be enlarged.
Focuses everyone's attention on what is being shown on a monitor.

Cons:
The presentation setup cost is approximately $3,000. However, leasing the equipment would be considerably cheaper.
Monitors or LCD and cables and connectors required.

Video Player

Pros:
Widely available.
Easy to operate.
The media can be shown on a regular TV monitor.

Cons:
Video production is expensive.
Must fast forward or rewind to get to a specific location. (However, if digitized, it can be played from a computer and any part can be instantly accessed).
Difficult to edit and annotate.

Graphs, charts, bullet slides, and other visual exhibits:

Pros:
Inexpensive to create, software packages start at $100.
Supports verbal points to the audience.
It can be displayed as a poster board, 35-mm slide, colored printout, transparency, slideshow presentation, etc.

Cons:
The display method may be expensive - depending on the choice.
Complexity may increase the cost.

Computer presentation software

(Display documents, graphics and/or video)

Pros:
It allows for instant flexibility in the retrieval of documents or graphics and lets you quickly shift from one document or graphic to the next.
Can draw everyone's attention simultaneously to specific parts of a document.
Can place documents side by side and enlarge.
Easy to annotate and save the annotation.
The cost of imaging documents and photographs are minimal.
It can synchronize video, audio, and documents together.

Cons:
Cost of setup.
Software costs - $100 - $1,000.
Computer equipment - can use your office computer equipment.
Presentation method - Monitors or LCD projector; renting or purchase can be expensive purchase $4,000 or up.

Scale Models

Pros:

It provides for a realistic three-dimensional view of the object, scene, etc.
It provides for a "picture" that may be worth a thousand words.

Cons:
Difficult to annotate.
Expensive.

Animations and Simulations

Pros:
It provides a two or three-dimensional view of the object, scene, etc.
Can view objects or scenes from many different viewpoints or angles.
It provides for a "moving picture" that may be worth a thousand words.

Cons:
Difficult to annotate.
Expensive.
Need to carefully lay the foundation for use in the presentation.

Now that we have some of the hardware out of the way, another type of "gear" that you need, on the tech side of things, is software to present with. This might include software like PowerPoint or some other slide software, video players, or a live software product. Make sure all software is updated and licensed. I usually recommend using purchased software instead of shareware. It is distracting and embarrassing for alerts to popup during your presentation that your software license has expired or that an update is due. Turn off all unnecessary programs. This will improve the performance and response of your device. For me, the worst culprit is Outlook reminders. Nobody cares about the remainder of your dog's birthday coming up as you are presenting.

Alright, now we have everything configured on your device. Next, you need a way to project all the good stuff from your device to where the audience can see it. I have used everything from an overhead projector plate to modern HD projectors. Again, the flip chart folks don't need to worry about this. A projector, connected to your device via a VGA or HDMI cable, is the most common tool used here. There are also wireless projectors that eliminate the need for the cable. I personally carry a 40-foot VGA and HDMI cable in my bag. Most projectors come with a cable measuring about 6 feet. I don't like being limited to positioning myself 6 feet from the projector, especially if I want to present from the front of the room. I also do not prefer presenting from behind everyone in the audience. This is the least effective position to present from. The long VGA cable is the best forty dollars that I ever spent. There are several places online where you can get a longer video cable. I got my cable from Cables.com.

Depending on the size of the room or number of attendees, another approach is to use a flat-screen TV or a large computer monitor. Remember to have appropriate cables and connectors in your bag.

Sometimes using a smaller screen creates a more intimate atmosphere for the presentation and encourages questions and discussion. I did a three-day series of presentations for a University Medical Center. One of our presenters had an emergency at home and had to leave the meeting. Being short a presenter I recruited another team member into filling the missing presenter's role. She was a nurse, so she had a medical background, but she had no presentation experience. The presentation was set in one of those big auditorium sized classrooms at the college with a lectern upfront. The nurse was very nervous about presenting in such a big room. I took a table and put it right up front with the audience and put a large flat screen monitor on the table. We had the attendees gather around the table and the nurse just sat down with them. She was able to just "talk" to them about the topic and was much more comfortable with the setup. It was rated one of the best topics presented during the 3-day event. She did a great job, we just had to create the right environment for her to succeed.

When you use a projector, another thing to think about is what you are projecting on. With a TV or monitor the images just get shown on the screen. With a projector, you need a flat surface in front of the projector, with no obstacles in the way. Many modern presentation rooms have automatic screens that come down from the ceiling. In a conference room, you can use a white dry erase board in a pinch. The problem is the dry erase board is reflective, i.e. the surface is not a flat color, so the projector light shines back on you. My preference is to project on a big white wall. During your discovery, when talking about the site for the meeting, an important question about the meeting space would be what is available to project on. You can also carry a projection surface with you. I have seen some very nice collapsible projection screens that can sit on the conference room table. The screens collapse into a tube or fold up and can be carried with you. If you mainly present in conference room environments, this might be a good option for you. Below is a picture of one of the tabletop projection screens.

One time, I arrived at a presentation in Louisville, Kentucky. The office manager escorted us back to the conference room to set up the presentation. Adorning the walls of the conference room was a two-tone, dark grey and purple velour wallpaper. There was no way to project on that. The salesperson had not done their job asking about our meeting space. We were in medical practice, so I went to one of the exam rooms and got some of the white paper from the exam room table. We proceeded to tape several layers of paper to the wall with masking tape. (I carry the tape in my gear bag). We created our own "screen" to project on. The stripes could still be made out under the paper, but it was tolerable.

In today's connected world part of your gear should be a connectivity solution. It is great when you arrive at the presentation site and there is a guest login to a wireless network set up for you. Again, this is a topic that needs to be discussed in advance if you need an internet connection. Many locations, like hotels, will charge you for connectivity. I don't count on having connectivity provided and I carry a wireless access point as a plan B. There are many standalone devices available. Many cell phones can turn into an access point. I try to have all my essential applications locally on my tablet, but it is good to have access in case you need to get on the internet or to perform an essential update or data transfer prior to the presentation.

Extension cords and power strips are another handy item in my gear bag. I carry a 10-foot extension cord. I purchased my extension cord from a home improvement store. It has 3 receptacles on one end, so it completes multiple roles as a power strip. I also carry a small 4 plug power strip with 2 plugs on each side. It is compact and the cord wraps around the plugs to conserve space.

I carry an external hard drive with backups of my databases and files. Basically, I could recreate my tablet environment from files on the backup drive. If the entire thing crashed, I could restore it.

In my computer bag, I carry a mesh goodie bag with all my necessary adapters, cords, plugs, small external speaker, flashlight, batteries, non-bladed multi-tool, plugs, etc. Outlet adaptors are handy because many old buildings still have 2 prong outlets. It is amazing how many difficult situations I get out of because I have my little bag of miscellaneous stuff. If I run into a situation where I need some small items, like an adaptor, I go out and buy that piece after the presentation. Then I always have it if that same situation occurs again.

I would encourage you to carry the universal fix-it. That's right, duct tape. Always have some in your bag. I carry duct tape, masking tape, and electrical tape. I get it in smaller rolls for portability. Duct tape has gotten me out of more jams than anything.

I was doing a presentation in Delaware at a hospital. We arrived at the conference room, and I positioned myself in front, and to the crowds left hand side. At that point, I found out that the room had a projector suspended from the ceiling, but the VGA port was on the wall in the back of the room. The consultant told me that everybody else just put their laptop on the back table and presented it from there. The back of the room is the worst position from which to present. So the big VGA cable came out of my bag, and I strung it from the VGA port, across the walkway, under the table, to my position at the front of the room. Next, the hospital IT guy came in and told me that I could not have the cable on the floor across where people were going to walk. He said he would have to call maintenance up to the conference room to "secure" it to the floor. I took my duct tape out of my bag and secured it myself. Everybody was happy and the presentation could proceed.

On the more unusual gear side, I used to carry a collapsible table. It had telescoping, locking legs that are stored in the body of the table. I used to put either my laptop or my projector on the table when I presented in larger auditoriums.

Another piece of gear that I carry in my bag is a pack of 3x5 cards. I use these for Q&A sessions, and to jot down outlines for parts of my presentation. I usually do not use notes or a written speech. I will jot down important points or a quick outline on 3x5 cards.

A device that I have seen used is a wireless presenter. These devices look like a remote control and allow you to run your slide show presentation via remote. There is a wireless transmitter that plugs into a USB port on the computer where the presentation is running. Some of the presenters have a laser pointer included with them. If you do a lot of slideshow presentations this tool would be a handy thing to have.

I usually have two of most things or I carry gear with duplicate functions. For example, my extension cord has multiple plugs on it and my power strip has a longer cord. Both could be used for an extension cord or power strip. To coin an old military mantra, "2 is 1 and 1 is none." Basically, this means if you have one of something and it stops working, or you lose it, you are out of luck. However, if you have a backup, you can still accomplish the task. Be as well prepared as possible with your equipment and do periodic checks and maintenance to make sure all your gear is in working order. I am constantly on the lookout for better, smaller, lighter, tougher gear and always welcome feedback and suggestions.

"Great, now I have all this stuff you want me to carry, now what do I put it all in?" I always look for a computer bag or a mobile office bag. I select a bag that will comply with airline regulations for carry-on and will fit under the seat. I do a lot of work on planes, so I like to have the bag under the seat in front of me instead of having to get up in the overhead bin. I do not like to check my bags. I don't want the fate of my presentation in the hands of the airline.

I prefer bags with wheels. I travel every week and wheeled bags just work better for me. I have talked with plenty of road warriors that take the backpack approach. I have carried a backpack and a shoulder bag and quite honestly prefer wheels. To each their own. Bags are a very personal preference and I have heard and understand arguments either way. I also prefer professional-looking bags in a neutral color. My last 10 or so bags have been black. During my presentation, I try to hide my bag and or equipment, but usually have my gear close by just in case I must grab that miscellaneous adapter.

I am kind of fanatical about organizing stuff in my bag. Everything has its place. I know where everything goes. Sometimes people offer to help me put stuff away and I must tell them no, because they will put something in the wrong spot. I have a mental checklist of all my presentation gear, so I make sure everything is accounted for.

Remember to test your equipment setup as early as possible and retest it just before the presentation. Follow a mental or written checklist for your equipment. Plan for the worst. Disasters will happen at some point, so have a backup plan. There is enough pressure to deliver information professionally and persuasively. You don't need the added anxiety of malfunctioning equipment.

Here is a little exercise for you. Create a list of all the technical things, hardware, software, equipment that has been missing, broken, crashed during any of your presentations, or any presentations that you have seen. Use this list to plan backup solutions or update your equipment. I do this all the time when I watch presentations. If I see something go wrong with some else's presentation, I will go and make sure I have a backup for whatever went wrong.

Chapter 2: Discovery

"All truths are easy to understand once they are discovered;
the point is to discover them."
Galileo Galilei

In the legal world, discovery is a term used for the pre-trial phase in a lawsuit, in which each party, through the law of civil procedure, can obtain evidence from the opposing party, by means of discovery documents that are filed with the court. In a court case, the two sides exchange facts and witness lists and evidence exhibit. This evens the playing field so neither side can pull a fast one. Neither party are allowed any surprises.

In presentations, especially sales presentations, discovery basically fills the same function. As a presenter, you need to gather facts to even the playing field and minimize surprises. The goal is to "discover" what is happening to the client, in an effort to understand their world and offer a solution to their problem. Discovery questions are great questions that provide the context we need to begin formulating a solution.

The term 'discovery' does have legal connotations, so I tend not to use that word with clients or prospects. Other names for discovery I have found include Customer Interview, Fact Finding, Pre-Presentation visit, Sales Interview, and Data Gathering.

Discovery is one of those differentiators in the sales process where you can still make an impression. Even when products are more of a commodity, people are not. Implementing and using sales tools for discovery during the sales process could be the difference between winning and losing a deal. Discovery is the key to understanding the issues your prospect is trying to resolve. The vendor with the most value to return is likely going to win the business.

I think the discovery phase is the single most important part of the entire sales process. If executed well, it is where the customer lays out the road map for how you can present a solution and win the deal. Yet too often, salespeople lose this opportunity, choosing to race through the process so they can get to the close.

Your primary goal in a sales discovery meeting is to learn about customer needs so you can maximize the effectiveness of your presentation and sales strategies later. For example, if you are selling a software program that streamlines database management, sales discovery meetings with office managers can help you identify which features of the software to highlight will address the prospect's needs. A shortlist of discovery topics might include:

1. Understand what the customer is trying to achieve and how this project relates to the attainment of their goals.

2. Understand what is driving the customer to change, or to consider something new. Why are they buying?

3. Understand what impact the issues have on the customer—both their business and the personal impact on everyone.

4. Understand who the prospect's competition is and how that affects their decision.

5. What other alternatives they are considering, why they are considering them, what they think about each of them.

6. Understand how they are going to decide. Who is involved? What are their roles? What each of their needs, issues, and priorities are?

7. Help them organize themselves toward deciding, to coach them how to buy.

8. Understand the impact of doing nothing.

9. Understand how the prospect will justify the implementation, or the purchase and where they will get the funding.

You need to learn what issues the prospect is trying to solve. What are the needs and or problems they are having? Why are they shopping? It is much easier presenting a proposed solution when you know what problem you are trying to solve. You could throw 10 solutions at them and hope the attendees recognize one of your solutions as something that will solve their problem. This is not a very productive or effective strategy.

By taking the time to question, probe, and learn, the customer gives you all the clues of what it takes to win. They give us the road map to success. Taking time to help the customer assess alternative approaches and to explore helps the customer discover new things that may be critical to their decision. Once we have guided the customer and ourselves through the process of discovery, presenting and selling becomes very simple. Just follow the roadmap.

Too many salespeople miss this. Instead, in their rush to propose, they know what product they must propose, but they don't have any other information to position their solution to show why the customer should select them. Since they haven't "discovered" everything about what the customer is seeking to do, they never address these issues. Consequently, it's up to the customer to figure it out. Unless the competition has helped them figure everything out because they took the time to truly discover.

The ultimate goal is to postpone pitching until you fully understand the prospect's need in terms that are both specific and measurable. Understandably, it is rare for complete and thorough discovery to take place before we succumb to pressure, whether that is from the prospect, our superiors, or our own impatience, to present a solution.

For me, the key metric is how long a salesperson can 'last' before entering their pitch. This is something we can

24

focus on and measure and improve upon. As with most skills or behaviors, simply drawing attention to the key metric puts you on the road to improvement. Start by measuring how long into your client-prospect conversation (measured in minutes) you can hold out before you find yourself telling them about yourself, your company, your product, and how you can help them. Notice your own natural 'pitch reflex', and don't beat yourself up when this happens. Instead, look for ways to redirect back to the discovery. When you find yourself rambling on about product features or easy financing options simply use a 'self-interrupt' technique to get back to asking questions. Nothing fancy, just stop yourself mid-sentence and try something like, "I'm getting ahead of myself. Please tell me more about your goals for your organization."

Digging for the problems or issues puts you into more of a consultative role with the prospect instead of just trying to sell them something. Discovery lets you find out what issues the customer is having so you can match your features and solutions to those issues for the presentation. This is a much more strategic approach. It's sniper sales. Find out the coordinates of your target first, so you can send munitions right to the target. Not to say you can't hit the target if you don't know where you are aiming, but it sure does increase the likelihood that your shot will be on the mark.

I have always recommended that discoveries be conducted in person. This gives you another touch with your prospects and allows you to strengthen the relationship. You might even develop a coach from the visit. Visiting the prospect in person also positions you as more of a consultant instead of the "salesperson." It increases your trust factor and allows the prospect to feel more confident about sharing information.

I will review some topics to help with your discovery process. This will build trust between you and your contact so getting more critical information out of them later, like info about your competition or their real budget, will be a lot easier.

1. Contacts and Decision Makers.

If you intend to get this information, it is best practice to get it right from the start. You might be eager to start "listening", which is critical in all discoveries, but your first order of business should be to establish the players and roles involved in authorizing a project. The importance of asking this question first is that it saves you the embarrassment of trying to scramble for it later. Finding out information about contacts and decision-makers lets you identify and hopefully turn a contact or multiple contact people into a champion and coach. If you start asking for other contacts late in the process, you risk losing their trust. You also lose the opportunity of making connections and targeting individual contacts throughout the sales and presentation process.

2. Listen.

The primary objective of the sales discovery process is listening to your customers or prospective customers. None of these other tips and tricks will really work that well if you don't listen to what the prospect is saying. Listening and documenting what you find out makes it easier when you are developing a presentation for the prospect. Sit back and let them tell you, their objective. If you have established any trust, the info that you thought you needed to pry out of them will be given freely. Some of my favorite questions after listening are:

1. What else?

2. Anything else you can think of that this solution needs to do?

3. Is that it?

4. And then?

These prompting questions will squeeze extra information and more detailed information from the discovery process. It is amazing how many times a question is answered very generally the first time and when you ask "what else" all the details come out.

3. Find that special thing.

What is the most important factor in their decision? As you are listening, your contact probably listed 10 things that are needed, that your solution is good at doing. Don't take the bait. Ignore all that. Those 10 features don't matter if you fail to determine what that one thing is that is important to this client or contact. It will be unique to them, and it is the thing that you focus on. If you can find one thing for each of the decision-makers and satisfy them in the presentation, that is about as good as it gets. An example question might look something like: "As far as moving this project forward is concerned, have you identified the most important thing the solution needs to do?" It is to your benefit that your software can do 10 things. If it can't do what is the most important thing for your contact or client, it won't matter if you can do 1,000 things better than the competition, they win. Most of the other salespeople will not ask for the one thing, so they never find it. So, if you find it and solve that important issue you will win most of the time. I will get the discovery sent to me from my sales team. When I review it, and I see generic answers with nothing specific, I will send it back and ask them to find me a way to win this. Historically, I have done presentations for products that were at the top of the food chain as far as price was concerned. Having a more expensive product basically forces you to sell value. Finding that key benefit goes a long way to justifying a bigger investment.

4. Identify impacts.

When you find out that unique item that you will focus on, identify how that problem impacts the contact. Is this problem just annoying? Does it cost them time during the day? Does it cost the contract or the company money? Does it affect the quality of the product that the company delivers? We can use the impacts of the presentation to reinforce our solution.

5. Timelines, Decision Date, Deadlines.

Great, so the customer just told you what they need in a solution. Now is the time to hit 'em with all the gee whiz-bang stuff your product can do and give them a great deal, right? WRONG. Now is the time to find out when and how the prospect wants to gather information about how your product can do those things. You can pose questions like:

a. If I can address your main objective with my solution, when is the right time to introduce it to your group?

b. What is the deadline for the project?

c. Does this fit in line with the Phase I user's availability to review a demonstration?

d. Does this fit into the timeline of when you review proposals and be able to select?

e. Does this fit in with the IT department's ability to support this project?

With these questions answered, you and your customer are now, and throughout the project, in a much better position to move through the evaluation and decision process as a team.

6. Explain the How.

Explain your process to the prospect, not your company and product. Again, I know you are anxious to talk about your product, your case studies, and customer testimonials. Be patient, there is plenty of time for all of that. Most of that will happen in the presentation. The presentation is the time to share your story. Remember, your customers most likely already did a little bit of recon, and they know you have products that can help. What the prospect cares about is more is how you help them. Your contact might not be on the end-user side of the solution. Maybe they care less about your product and care more about something else. That is something else you should know by now, right? Thoroughly explain the members of your team and all the resources you will bring to the table during the process of introducing your product to the organization. Offer various presentation models to present your solution (webinars, demonstrations, quotes, case studies, statements of work, etc.) and let the prospect tell you how they want you to provide it. Your customer will place much higher trust in you and respect the amount of time and energy you are devoting to their problem and rely on your method vs. the competition.   If you make it easier for the prospect to do business with you, most often they will.

7.   Set the next appointment.

Successfully consulting a prospect through a project-oriented purchase is about getting a series of positive commitments. Setting the next appointment is really all that you need to aim for because of the first call. If your next appointment is in line with the project's timeline, you have passed the first test to see if you have established trust and you've mastered the keys to an effective discovery call. The next appointment might be the presentation to the board. It all starts with proper discovery.

An essential part of the discovery is asking questions. It would be great if you just show up and the prospect just told you everything you need to know. In the discovery process, I believe nothing is more important than

29

learning to ask the right questions of a prospect. Some basic discovery questions might include:

1. What are they trying to accomplish with their new product or services?

2. How would they use your product or services?

3. What products or services have they been using?

4. What did they like the best about their previous product or service?

5. What did they like the least about their previous product or service?

6. If they could design the perfect product or service, how would they do it? What options or features would it have?

7. What is wrong with the product or services that they are using now?

For your situation, product, and industry, discovery questions will vary. Each salesperson and presenter will have to develop their own discovery questions, over time, to be most successful.

Effective questions get the customer to think of things differently. Questions allow them to consider other options, or to shift their point of view. The whole tone of a discovery meeting changes when the customer says, "I've never thought about that," or "I didn't realize that was possible," or "No one has ever asked me that before." There are many different types of questions to use during discovery. Let's take a minute and review the types of questions and their uses. These question types include Opening questions, Closing questions, Direct questions and Provoking questions.

The first type of discovery meeting question is called Opening Questions. I have also heard them called Open-Ended Questions. During your visit begin with open-ended questions. This allows customers the flexibility to expound and provide detailed accounts of their needs. Let them do it. I know many salespeople that will interrupt and start solving the problem. Use the open-ended questions and let the customer talk. Your job is to listen. For example, ask for a general breakdown of current problems and the customer's opinion about available solutions. This interview approach stimulates a free-form discussion rather than a stiff question-and-answer session. In other words, steer conversations toward fertile areas, but do so in a way that allows customers to explain all their concerns.

Opening questions also allow you to find the common thread. During your first few meetings, you will probably have a rough idea of what customers are looking for. As you continue to interview people, you'll notice common threads. For example, you might notice most customers think a certain user interface is hard to use. Identifying these ubiquitous sentiments helps you tailor sales strategies to impact a larger population of your potential customer base. So, discovery can not only be valuable for the current deal but for future deals as well.

The next discovery meeting question is a Closing Question. Use Closing Questions toward the end of the meeting. Narrow your questions to obtain the specific information you need. As an example, you might ask if the customer would be interested in a solution like the one your company offers at a price point. Keeping close-ended questions until the end allows you to obtain the affirmative or negative answer, you're looking for without stifling enlightening conversation too early. Closing questions are generally limited in their answer. Yes and No questions are closing questions.

Direct Questions focus on The Who, What, Where, Why, How. They are designed to identify existing customer problems, needs, pain points, goals, etc. Direct Questions are designed to get to the known, present facts and to ferret out what the customer knows about their environment.

31

Examples of Direct Questions are:

1. What are you currently challenged with?

2. What are you trying to accomplish?

3. What happens when you miss XYZ?

4. How will you be measuring success?

5. What have been the results to date?

6. Are you happy with your current environment?

7. What tools are you currently using?

Direct questions are also good for obtaining an impact. You may have an opening question that lets the customer give lots of information and then follow it with a direct question.

Provoking Questions are the last kind of discovery question. Provoking questions take questioning to the next level. Provoking questions are designed to challenge the customer and get them thinking in ways they had not thought of. Provoking questions are designed to get into the thinking processes and the logic behind their choices. These questions provide insight into what the customer or prospect knows, what they don't know and what they prioritized to make their decisions. Provoking questions help you and your customer or prospect evaluate what they are doing and why. Some examples of Provoking questions are:

1. Were you aware that . . . ?

2. Did you know . . . ?

3. Have you thought about . . . ?

4. Can I ask why you . . . ?

5. Have you seen . . . ?

6. Would you . . . ?

7. What was the reason behind . . . ?

Provoking questions are designed to get the customer or prospect to think outside of the proverbial box. To be able to respond to great questions from the salesperson, the customer must put structure, definition, and priorities around what they are trying to achieve. Great questions can help the customer think about how they will make the decision.

Ask all four types of discovery questions. Go deep, get to the nitty-gritty. Challenge your customers or prospects to self-evaluate. The more you get them thinking about their choices and why they are doing what they are doing, the more they're going to come to you for direction and guidance.

By asking these discovery questions, your clients are going to tell you exactly how to sell them. However, you don't want to start selling them or trying to solve their problems during the discovery process, because it is just a fact-finding time. Just avoid selling and solving during discovery. If you try and sell after each question, they will stop telling you this valuable information. The prospect will realize that you are using their answers against them, and they won't answer you with the truth. Take detailed notes so you don't forget what they told you. Once you have this information you will design your presentation around the needs of your clients as you show them how your product or service will solve all their problems. As a sales professional, you are looking to find a need so you can present a solution. If you're selling, you're not listening and learning. Save the selling until later when you know the lay of the land.

Another discovery technique is performing personal interviews. Perhaps you do not have a contact person, or do not have the time to create, implement, and analyze a valid discovery survey. This does not mean there is nothing you can do to gather more data on your audience. One final strategy you may employ is to personally interview potential audience members to allow you to gauge their interest in your topic, and perhaps, their actual opinion on the matter. If you know the person whom you interview, you also might get information on other potential audience members that can be quite useful, especially in a sales situation. Interviews also have the bonus of allowing you to get to know someone who will attend your talk. Knowing someone in the audience can help reduce tension and anxiety when you deliver your remarks. It also allows you to catch up with that person at the event before you talk to see if there is any other information, he or she can relay to you. Interviews are an intensely personal matter for several reasons. First, you are asking people to give time from their day to speak with you, and this in and of itself is a big commitment. Second, you are asking them to use that time to share their personal attitudes, beliefs, and ideas with you so you should respect them for sharing that information, even if it might not be what you wanted or expected to hear. Finally, interviews usually occur in one-on-one settings, whether it is in-person, over the phone. Nonverbal behaviors that convey information regarding a person's personality will be available. This information must not be abused.

When you get to the demonstration or presentation phase of your sales process be sure you are presenting the solution to the issues, pains and goals identified and agreed upon during discovery. I love showing all the cool and new features, but believe me, you will lose the audience. It also tends to make the contact a little angry that they spent all this time with you sharing information and none of that data was used in the presentation.

Another benefit of discovery is as a qualifying tool. There is a saying in sales "If you can't win, lose early." In other words, you don't want to waste significant time, money and energy getting deep into the sales process and perform the big presentation, only to find out that your product was not actually what the prospect was looking for.

Your mission in discovery is, of course, to identify issues, pains, and goals, determine the current cost of the status quo and decide to move forward or not. At the same time, an objective for you is to make sure the deal is a potential fit. Without this goal an opportunity is not always an opportunity, it's a distraction. Why is the prospect talking to you? Did they agree to meet with you because an inside sales rep harassed them until they said yes, and they just don't want to be cold called anymore? Do they want a free lunch at the local restaurant, or do they have a problem that they need help with? There are a lot of tire kickers out there and you owe it to yourself to find out who they are. No need to go into a long sales cycle with someone who wanted the free lunch and now feels bad saying 'no' to you.

I see this all the time where the salesperson just is trying to make the prospect happy. This is when the salesperson just does not want to say no to the prospect. I got a request to do a presentation a few weeks ago where the salesperson was asking me to present a product that we don't even have. I conducted a discovery phone call with the salesperson and prospect. Examining the prospects' needs revealed that they were looking for a completely different solution to what my company offered. At least we found this out early instead of on-site in front of a lot of people.

The worst case of non-discovery-itis happened a few years ago. A medical practice was looking to replace their practice management software. The practice was using a consultant for the evaluation. The consultant contacted our salesperson to say that the practice wanted a presentation. The salesperson rushed into the presentation and did not do any discovery. When I got to the demonstration, I started asking questions before just launching into my presentation. It turned out that this practice was an existing customer. They were looking for a new system, to replace us! That might have been handy to know beforehand.

Discovery is a great process for bringing out potential red flags. During your discovery, you should see some distinctive behaviors from your client or prospect. These behaviors might include:

1. Believes your offering is valid

2. Understands your value

3. Wants to pull in influencers and other decision-makers

4. Shares information with you

5. Wants to set up the next step

5. Asks you questions based on your expertise

Not seeing any of these behaviors constitutes a red flag that you need to look out for. When these behaviors are not being displayed, I think it is better to part friends and spend time presenting to prospects that have the potential of generating business. In my opinion, the discovery call is for both parties to learn about each other and not a groveling session where you kiss up and agree to everything your prospect asks. Remember that you are the expert and carry yourself as such. Be honest, have confidence in your solution and sell like you don't need the business.

The logistics of the presentation also need to be part of the discovery process. Where will the presentation take place? Can we look at the room in advance? How many attendees? What equipment is available? These questions are examples of logistics discovery:

Questions and tips that should be considered regarding the meeting room's facilities:

1. Does it have Wi-Fi capability?

2. Are there wired computer hookups? How many?

3. Where are the electrical outlets?

4. Is there a built-in sound system?

5. How are the acoustics in the room?

6. Check the room for exterior noise.

7. How is the lighting for the presenter and audience and how is the lighting controlled?

8. Can windows be covered with shades, blinds, or curtains?

9. What support is provided for maintenance problems or additional equipment needs and who to contact?

10. Is the meeting room accessible before the meeting for setup?

11. Are different seating arrangements available to support the event and presenter's goals?

12. Are surfaces available for writing, using manuals, laptops, and placing beverages?

13. Are accommodations available for people with special hearing, seeing or mobility needs?

14. Is there easy access to seating with an adequate number and width of aisles?

15. Is the space proportionate to the number of people attending?

16. Check for adequate air control and comfortable air temperature.

17. Find out if water, coffee, or other refreshments will be provided

18. Test equipment for working order (video, projectors, monitors).

19. Note the proximity to restrooms and coat storage.

20. See that exit doors are clearly marked.

Who is attending the meeting? This is one of the most important questions for me. I want to get at least a general idea of who is going to be attending. Maybe this meeting will just have the C-suite in attendance, or the department managers, or the end-users. You would give a different presentation or a different view of the material depending on what type of attendees are in the room. For example, the C-suite attendees usually react better to bottom-line numbers and corporate vision, while department managers would be more concerned with workflow and how the solution would affect end users.

Use the discovery process either before or during the meeting to identify audience members. For each member identify needs or at least their top problem that need solving. For each issue, identify impacts.

If given my choice, I prefer an attendee list in advance. On the attendee list, I like at minimum the person's name, title, and contact information. In addition, I would like to get some main points that the attendees are looking to see in the presentation. When you get this detailed information in advance, you can customize the presentation to address the needs of each attendee. I have done presentations where we have passed a signup sheet around. That is good information to have, but you usually only get to see the completed signup sheet after the presentation. So, you don't have a chance to adjust the presentation based on attendee needs. With larger presentations, you might collect the information about attendees by role, instead of individually. Another option would be to get more detailed information on the individuals in the C-suite and the rest of the details by the group. For example, If the CFO is the person writing the check and the only issue, they care about is "x" then I am going to make sure and work "x" into the presentation. In the presentation, you need to present the features that address the needs and tie them down to your findings from our discovery.

If the discovery is completed, I should have something that every audience member or group wants to see, so I can create a presentation where everyone gets a win.

After each presentation, I always look to see what I could have done better. Most of the time if something happened during the presentation that could have been handled better, it will come down to discovery. I will ask myself:

1. Did I really understand their issues?

2. Was I able to help the prospect determine their true cost of the status quo?

3. Was I able to get the prospect to agree on the on-going cost of the status quo and the cost of decision delay?

4. Did I really understand their tipping point or threshold for pain?

These four magical discovery questions and the answers will reduce a great deal of your anxiety in the sales process and shed light on your performance during debriefing the presentation.

Being adept at discovery has been invaluable in my career and in my life. Once you understand the process it is applicable in various aspects both professionally and personally. A job interview is a good example. This is basically a presentation, but instead of presenting a product or service, you are presenting yourself. You might do research on the company or on the position. You could talk to other employees. check out the company website. You are doing research or discovery on the company to help you prepare for the interview. Understanding the questioning and discovery process allows you to tackle a lot of situations with more confidence.

Chapter 3: Coaches

"A coach is someone who can give corrections without causing resentment.
John Wooden

Coaches are invaluable for a presentation, especially for a sales presentation. Coaches are basically people on the inside of the organization that you are speaking to that can give you all kinds of information during the discovery process and on an ongoing basis. These coaches are individuals who provide accurate information about the sales cycle, corporate culture, personalities of the major players, issues, goals, fears hidden agendas, and even competition. A great coach will not only provide intel but will help promote and represent a salesperson's solution to his colleagues or to senior leadership. Many times, the coach can give you a few softball questions during the presentation that can be answered positively. Coaches can be found during the discovery process and nurtured throughout the sales process. Often, I have seen that the coach is someone in the organization that has used your solution before.

Coaches are also referred to as Internal Champions. For most sales situations, a lot of selling and decision making can occur when you're not there. Salespeople need someone to "tell their story" when they can't be there to tell it. And they are not there most of the time. Because of that fact, top salespeople are adept at developing internal champions. Getting an internal coach is a must-have versus a nice-to-have. Changes occur all the time – what was true yesterday may not be true today. In such an environment, you absolutely need someone who has a seat at the table who can sell for you when you are not there and keep you up to speed.

Internal champions are crucial to discovery, preparing the presentation and winning key business. When it comes to the time to do the presentation for the group, the presentation becomes more of a confirmation of the ideas

41

that have already been sold internally. If the presentation is the first time that the audience hears about a new idea or solution, they will not be as accepting. If the group has already been introduced to the idea by the coach, audiences are much more receptive.

I found a particularly effective definition of an internal champion from a Harvard Business Review blog by Steve Martin. Internal champions "are confidants who provide all the inside details about the internal politics of decision making, but they also help you plan and execute your strategy to win the business."

Coaches sound great so why don't we use a coach on every presentation that we perform? First, some salespeople fall into the trap of trying to develop the wrong people into the coach. They spend time with people who are "willing" to be their internal champion but are not "able" to tell their story when the salesperson is not there. Those coaches can have little effect on advancing the sale. They could even have a negative effect if the "wrong" person is the internal champion. You must be very careful about who you select to get the appropriate affect. Next, developing internal champions is time and resource consuming. Not every salesperson wants to invest time and effort. Walking into a presentation having discovery and that internal champion on your side instills a lot of confidence.

So now knowing that a coach is valuable for the sale and the presentation, the question is, how do you go about developing them? Unfortunately, there's no map to follow, but a couple of strategies to are:

1. Meet many people at a company before deciding on whom to develop as an internal champion.

2. Develop more than one internal champion in an account. For example, have a coach in IT, end-users, management, C-suite, etc.

3. Jointly develop a strategy to introduce your product or service

4. Create a situation where the result of being your internal champion is a "win" for them, too.

5. Commit the appropriate amount of time to develop your internal coach.

6. Realize that competitors might also have internal champions.

7. Rehearse with your internal champion. It is almost always true that internal champions do not have selling skills and it is always true that they do not know as much about your solutions and company as you do. So, if they are to sell for you effectively, then rehearsing becomes a big deal. Rehearsing is probably the most poorly executed of all the requirements of developing and managing internal champions.

Now that we have some ideas about developing a coach, what characteristics should you look for in such a person? According to a report by The Sales Executive Council (SEC) developing internal champions is important to the sales process. The SEC identified six characteristics of an internal champion or coach:

1. Is accessible

2. Speaks the truth and can provide valuable information typically unavailable to suppliers

3. Is pre-disposed to support the supplier's solution

4. Is credible and effective at presenting to and influencing others

5. Has some personal skin in the game (advocates much more likely to help if they stand to profit themselves)

6. Can network reps with other customer stakeholders and actually delivers on commitments.

7. I would add a seventh characteristic to the SEC report. To be effective, an internal champion not only has to be willing to be your champion, but they also must be a player in decision making. People you develop as champions cannot be of any benefit if they do not have decisive authority. In a complex sale, this is an easy trap to fall into as it's often difficult to determine the true decision-making authority or influential power that various players possess.

The more of these traits that a potential coach has, the better, but many times all these characteristics don't exist in a single person. Sometimes a salesperson will seek out and engage multiple coaches. Accessibility and eagerness are necessary traits and the easiest to come by, but not sufficient. These accessible and eager people don't have what it takes to advance the sale and promote the solution. A coach must be able to build consensuses within the buying organization and sell when the salesperson isn't there. The coach must be marketing and promoting the solution internally.

The coach could be anybody inside the customer's company, or even outside the company, such as a consultant working on the project. All these advisors share a common characteristic. They have a reason for wanting you or your company to win. This reason may range from the simple fact that they like you, to the complicated nature of politics, where your solution helps them gain power, prestige, or authority. I have seen many situations where I have had a consultant as a coach and the win for the consultant was that they were going to get more consulting work if our solution was selected.

Developing true internal champions takes substantial time and effort. The salesperson needs to apply stringent criteria in who they engage and select to play the role of internal champion or coach. The ideal coach is the person with the highest authority or influence involved in the selection process. When this person becomes your coach, you will enjoy a unique advantage.

The more coaches you have inside an account, the better the quality and quantity of information you will receive. In fact, it is a smart strategy for engaging multiple coaches. Being at the mercy of a single person is a risky position to be in. With multiple coaches, you can compare the information that you received for consistency. The information you get from these coaches can be used to determine your standing in an account and help determine your course of action.

Sometimes salespeople think they have a coach when, in reality, they don't. There are five different types of coaches who bring different values to the table in a sales situation. Understanding the different types of coaches helps the salesperson know if they have a true coach or not.

1. Frenemy.

A person who is ostensibly friendly or collegial with someone but who is antagonistic or competitive. A frenemy is someone who befriends you so that you think they are a supporter. The frenemy is only acting the part and is truly working against you. Frenemies are extremely dangerous because they lull you into a false sense of security that you are winning the sale when they are really coordinating a plan to defeat you.

2. Well-Wisher.

A well-wisher talks to you on a trusting and friendly basis. They provide information that you consider proprietary. The well-wisher, however, is an extremely amiable person and is probably providing the same information to all the salespeople competing for the business.

3. Weak Spy.

Weak spies are observers who provide you information about the internal politics of the selection process. They report the thoughts of the various selection team members and keep you informed on the progress of other vendors.

4. Strong Spy.

Strong spies are not only observers but also disseminators of information. They promote you and your solution to others within their company when you aren't around. Strong spies have a deeper, more personal connection to you than weak spies do. They're more akin to confidants than acquaintances.

5. Guide.

Guides are trusted friends who will courageously defend you and your solution since they have a vested interest in your winning. Guides can be considered best friends. Not only are they confidants who provide all the inside details about the internal politics of decision making, but they also help you plan and execute your strategy to win the business. Guides are usually seasoned employees. They've worked at the company for quite some time and understand how to get things done. They have the business acumen and the experience to provide adept advice on how to win the deal and get the contract signed. Most importantly, after helping devise the wining game plan, they play an integral part in executing it. Really a Guide is the only type of coach that can be considered a true internal champion.

You should always have a certain level of caution about your coach. Some things to be aware of are:

1. Is the coach secretly coaching the competition?

2. Is the coach acting as your eyes and ears when you are not around?

3. Is the coach truthfully telling you about what the other vendors are up to and about the preferences of the various selection committee members?

4. Is the coach providing privileged and proprietary information to you that the other vendors aren't receiving?

What do you do when your coach inside a prospective company decides to leave just as you were collecting information to make a presentation? Selling and presenting in the B2B world is very difficult and time-consuming. There is so much information you need to have to make the above determinations. If your champion leaves during the sales process, you must be sure you have collected all the information during your time together. You also want to ensure you have been introduced to other stakeholders within the organization. If you have a true Guide in the organization, your coach will probably give you a fair warning of what is happening. I have had coaches leave and introduce me to their replacement in the organization, so I could start to enlist them as the next coach.

Maybe a better question is how well did you perform discovery when you had the opportunity to talk with someone inside the organization? Did you make the best of your time? There is no substitute for a good discovery process. A good discovery is an insurance policy against things happening like your coach leaving. I have had coaches leave, move to other departments, even fired.

A completed and ongoing discovery document and process is the key to overcoming the loss of your champion. If you can collect key information each time you interact with your prospect and make the determination early in the process that you have a solution, then it won't be or shouldn't be fatal if your champion leaves. Especially if you can return a report verifying the data you collected to the replacement. The key once again is the quality and amount of data you have collected during discovery.

Your guide is essential in gauging where the prospective customer is in their process. The coach can inform the salesperson when the prospect is nearing their decision point. I think of the sale like a bell curve, with Interest in you and your products on the vertical axis and time is on the horizontal axis. As the sale progresses a prospect's interest increases. At some point in the process, they have what they want and need, and interest begins to decline. You want to provide information to fuel the prospect up the incline and do the presentation almost at the top. If you don't close the sale before the decline gets too far down the backside of the bell curve, your chances of closing will be significantly reduced.

Prospects are looking for all the information on your products and services they can get, a demo or presentation, and the price. After that, they are either going to move forward and buy, continue looking at your competition, or they are going to do nothing. I believe it is a little thing called a "tipping point." The tipping point is the point where an organization realizes the costs of the pain are too much to continue to handle. Now the benefits of a solution will likely outweigh the costs. The key to this statement is that you and your prospect agree on the cost and value that can be delivered. Your coach can give you guidance about where you are on the hill and assist in slowing or quickening the ascent or descent. I have many sales completed by the coach calling up the salesperson and saying "OK we are there. We are ready to go." That is a great coach or guide that will call to alert you to the fact that the prospect is teetering at the tipping point.

Another key benefit of an internal coach is when it comes time to make a business case. This usually involved dealing with the C-Suite. The coach can validate the discovery along with the value. The coach will ensure you are always on the same page with the prospect.

I believe there are a few consistent truths when dealing with business-to-business sales that the coach can assist you with:

1. You will likely have to deal with the C-Suite (Likely a finance person)

2. You will have to provide financial validation and justification

3. To be effective you must be able to articulate your value in terms of economic impact

4. You will have to produce a Business Case

The one factor all four of these points have in common is their reference to something relating to finance. The C-Suite speaks a language of their own that is typically foreign to the average sales professional. They communicate with each other and the outside world in terms like economic impact, budgets, and earnings per share. They have ratios they keep a very close eye on, and they are always looking at the impact a purchase will have) on their cash flow. Your coach can guide and help with what information the C-Suite is looking for in a presentation or business case.

Before meeting with the C-Suite you must be very well prepared. Wasting their time will likely be fatal. As part of your preparation, your discovery with the coach must include questions about the ratios they use to make strategic buying decisions. Don't be afraid to ask questions like, "What ratios do you use to evaluate a major purchase?" You may ask about the process they use to make a buying decision and what impact, if any does a Business Case has on it. To be sure you can express economic impact in terms of their ratios it is crucial you understand your value impact will affect prospects financials. There is the additional step of applying your value to the issue and measuring the economic impact, then converting the impact into a ratio your prospect will understand and appreciate.

The bottom line on this one is that you need to use your coach and great discovery questions to identify issues, pains, and goals. Next, you will need to capture the cost or potential revenue losses that directly relate to the issues defined. Finally, establish your value and measure the impact. These measurements as part of your discovery process will then be used in your Business Case and proposal.

When you are presenting to the C-Suite it is critical that you understand these facts. If you expect to be successful when presenting to the C-Suite, you must learn and speak their language. You must be able to articulate your value in terms of economic impact and using their ratios.

If you are lucky enough to have your coach in the C-Suite, then the process of presenting and selling to them is much shorter and easier. Sometimes this is called an Executive Sponsor when you have a C-Suite coach.

Selling and presenting in the business-to-business space is more difficult than it has been in a very long time. Times have changed and buyers have changed the way they buy. Buyers know more about solutions, options, and opportunities that put the seller on the defense. The world market has opened up and brought with it a lot more competition. Having and using coaches give you an advantage in navigating the companies processes and obtaining information critical to the presentation and ultimately the sale.

Chapter 4: Presentation Prep - Building the Presentation

"It usually takes more than three weeks to prepare a good impromptu speech."
Mark Twain

Now that you have spent significant time on the discovery, and you have your coach to help you the key information, let's put that work to use in preparing the presentation for the audience. The key to preparing your presentation is the identification of the specific needs or critical business issues of your audience.   Find out what your presentation needs to look like.   Ask your contact or coach "If I give the perfect presentation, what will the audience know that they didn't know before." How is the audience better off by spending time with me? You are asking for the target. What do I need to hit to consider this a win? You need to know what is expected. Then, you can laser focus on giving them what they want. This can be part of the discovery process. A presentation reflects you and your work. You want to make the best possible impression in the short amount of time given to you. An effective presentation not only requires good content but also requires a good way to deliver it, so as to maintain the interest of the audience. I divide my preparation into phases. The phases in my preparation include:

1. Phase 1 - Define
2. Phase 2 - Gather
3. Phase 3 - Compose
4. Phase 4 - Practice
5. Phase 5 - Adjust

This chapter will concentrate mostly on Phases 1, 2 and 3. I will make some general comments about Phase 4 and 5 in this chapter, but I have separate chapters on Practicing and Debriefing for more details.

Define

The first phase of building the presentation is the definition, or the Define Phase you will use all the information that you collected in the discovery. The presentation should be based on the discovery data.

You have probably heard of the term WIIFM (What's In It For Me). For presentations, you need to think about this in terms of WIIFA (What's In It For the Audience). Always be thinking about this in the back of your head as you define and develop your presentation. Think from the audience's perspective and ask yourself "So what?" Remember from the discovery process the audience or audiences that you are addressing. The "So what?" for one part of the audience might not be the same as another.

You will need to target your presentation to suit your audience. This means that you will need to analyze your audience. What characteristics do they possess which may be important to your presentation? Are they a specific demographic, professional group, cultural, interest group? Why is the audience coming to see the presentation? What expectations does the audience have? Is there any sensitive issue that you should be aware of? Is the audience likely to be supportive or hostile toward your point of view? What does your audience really want from you? You might think this is all about you, but people don't go to presentations to see you. They care about what they can get from you. Know what that is and offer it. Your task is to know what the audience wants to get from you and use it to design your offering. What presentation method will be most effective with the audience you are targeting?

You need to nail the benefit. To get a good response from your audience, the presentation needs to have a clear benefit. It's important to formulate the benefits right from the start. Also, decide what they'll walk away with. What will they be able to do, think, or feel as a result of your presentation? Choose one to three takeaways. If you give too much, people will get overwhelmed and use nothing. If you give too little, they'll remember nothing but your sequined bell-bottoms.

Armed with this knowledge of what you want the audience to take away, you're much more likely to be able to put together a presentation that is relevant for your audience. But is it relevant to you? That's an important point. Let's go ahead and ask another set of questions.

What do you want to achieve with the presentation? What is the overall goal? Determine the purpose of your presentation and identify your own objectives. Are you aiming to:

1. Educate and inform
2. Inspire/interest and persuade
3. Entertain
4. All of the above

The style of presentation may differ depending on your purpo se. My vote would be for option #4. The goal of Infotainment is to convey information, inspire action and entertain at the same time. Identify your goal for the presentation. You must meet your needs, too. Prepare for that in advance. You want this to be a win/win experience. Otherwise, you'll end up with a happy audience, and an unhappy presenter.

I have seen presenters do an exceptional job at presenting, but then not have business cards or put any contact information in the presentation. Especially for a sales-oriented presentation. If the audience wants to take the action that you are calling for, they need an outlet to do that.

As you start preparing your talk, you need to decide who your audience is and what your message will be. The message must grab and hold attention. What idea do you want the audience to be repeating as they leave the room? What idea do you want them to tell their friends about? Messaging needs to be tailored to the audience. Messaging should be offensive, not defensive. In other words, the message must emphasize the company and solution strengths and advantages. A good speaker focuses the speech on one simple message that is easy to understand. You don't want your audience to get lost with too many levels of detail.

How do you decide the main message of your presentation? Begin with the end in mind. Start preparing with a few simple questions with the audience benefit in mind. Start with your key talking points. There's no point in writing a full script or presentation until you know what points you want to hammer home. Then, you can stick with a standard format:

1. Tell them what you are going to tell them

2. Tell them

3. Tell them what you told them

What is your story thread? Whatever the topic of your presentation is, it's sometimes useful to consider using a consistent story thread or motif. We have internalized many archetypal motifs through stories that have been told and retold through the generations. There are many more such story threads. If you use a story thread, your presentation will be strengthened with an invisible backbone. A consistent motif will make it easy to find appropriate metaphors and images to support your topic.
A few examples of a story motif:

1. Good vs. Evil
2. Overcoming difficulties
3. The reluctant hero
4. Voyage into the unknown
6. Finding the source
7. The blockbuster story

You can structure your talk so that it is memorable for you as well as for your audience. A structure that storytellers have used since ancient times is the three-act

54

form. In keeping with the underlying three-act structure, you need three main building blocks, the opening, the development, and the closing.

In the design of your presentation, Act 1 is the opening. It is the description of the pain points, challenges, and frustration that your audience faces with respect to your topic. When you promise to show how to overcome these challenges in order to reach the desired outcome, you set up dramatic tension.

The corresponding part of your presentation is Act 3. It offers the resolution and describes how one is changed and rewarded through overcoming challenges and attaining the desired outcome. Act 2 is the detailed description of the path from A to B. It is the 'how to' section of the presentation.

No matter what your topic is, this structure ensures that you connect with your audience, because people feel understood when you name their pain, and inspired when you show them how to overcome it. This three-act structure ensures dramatic tension and release, which you need to create a memorable presentation.

Most presenters these days use PowerPoint slides or some other slideshow application. That can be very effective because you can use images and motion to hammer home your points. I think in general PowerPoint presentations are great if you want to convey information. However, if your presentation revolves is inspirational and revolves around your personal story, then just words may well work better because such a presentation is more intimate. Whether or not you use PowerPoint, it's important for your presentation to sound like your talking, and not reading aloud. Don't let technology dominate the presentation. You want the audience to remember the quality of your research, not your PowerPoint wizardry.

Another thing to keep in mind when defining your presentation is how much time do you have available to talk?

This will have implications in terms of how much detail you are able to cover. As a matter of courtesy and good planning, try to stick to your allotted time.

Gather

Once you have defined what you want to do for your presentation, the next step is gathering data. Research is one of my favorite parts of the process. When I need to learn about new topics for myself, I basically do the exact same process as if I was going to do a presentation. I just don't do the presentation at the end.

Ensure that you understand the assignment topic and have access to a suitable range of relevant references. Do sufficient background reading to ensure that you are fully familiar with the topic being covered and sufficient to enable you to field questions from the audience if required. Make sure that the scope of the talk is clearly defined in your discovery process. How much detail do you need? Remember, your time and your audience's attention are limited. For any part of your presentation, ask yourself "So what?"

Brainstorming presentations by understanding the audience's point of view is not easy, but I think it is essential in gathering information for your presentation. We will examine a simple process to create a presentation from an audience's point of view.

The first step in brainstorming for audience needs is that you need to know the answer to the question. What are the audience's needs? This information comes from the discovery that was collected.

I will create a grid on a legal pad or create a spreadsheet for my brainstorming. First, write down all the needs that you uncovered during the discovery process. In the next column, I list the features, functions, and services of the solution that address those needs. The next column is the benefit. How does solving the need benefit the audience? The benefit needs to be as much concrete data as possible. In other words, the benefit needs to be expressed in something that the audience can get their heads around. Time savings decreased costs; increased revenues are examples of concrete benefits. Lastly, I created an evidence column. This could be a case study or a quote from an existing customer that achieved the same result or the average benefit from the customer base.

I have seen another example of this type of method recently called the SCORE Method. The SCORE method is as follows:

S-Situation
Co-Complication
R-Resolution
E-Example

The next method to brainstorm your presentation, for audience needs, is the concept of the Final Person. The Final Person is the last person that needs to act to take the next step in the decision-making process. That person might be the executive that has to sign off on the project or the consultant that will recommend the solution to the board. First, you need to find out who the final person is. Again, this could be a key question in the discovery process. Imagine that you are the last person, who needs to take the Next step as defined in your presentation objective. Note down your thoughts. Start writing down all the questions you want to be answered as the 'final person', to take the next step. This process helps you move away from the traditional ME to YOU (presenter's point of view) style of presenting to the recommended YOU to ME style of presenting.

An example of a Final Person brainstorming session might look like this. Let's assume that you are a database designer pitching for a development project for a small company. The last person is the owner of the business. The next step is signing a contract with you for the project. The questions that might arise during this phase from the owner of the business are:

1. Does the vendor understand my business-specific problems?

2. Will the vendor waste my time and money?

3. How can I believe that the vendor will deliver great results?

4. Will the project take too much of my time and attention?

5. Does the vendor know enough to give me suggestions, or will they just follow my suggestions?

6. Will the vendor be too expensive?

7. Can I do this myself at a lower cost?

8. Will there be recurring costs for maintenance?

9. Who else has the vendor worked with, in my industry?

10. How good is the after-sales service?

These were just a few questions from the top of the mind. The more time you take, the deeper you get and come up with some real concerns. As you can see, such a presentation starts with your listener's concerns in mind and will, therefore, be more remarkable. The What Is In It For Me (audience) flows right through your presentation. When you answer these questions through a brainstorm session, your presentation almost creates itself.

Next Step: Creating the 'Concern Areas' sheet:

Now that you have a list of audience-specific items from your brainstorming session, we need to categorize, organize and label these questions to make a storyboard, which is ready to be converted into slides. When you take a closer look at the questions, you would realize that the questions can be grouped based on the broad concern areas.

In the brainstorming examples above I could group them into several categories:

Cost

1. Will the vendor waste my time and money?

2. Will the project be too expensive?

3. Can I do this myself at a lower cost?

4. Will there be recurring costs for maintenance?

5. Does the vendor understand my business-specific problems?

Experience

1. How can I believe that the vendor will deliver great results?

2. Will the project take too much of my time and attention?

3. Does the vendor know enough to give me suggestions, or will they just follow my suggestions?

4. Who else has the vendor worked with, in my industry?

5. How good is the after-sales service?

As you can see, we quickly generated ideas for the presentation and put them into thought-groups in a very short span of time.

When you do your research, take notes as you go to be used later to construct your presentation notes. Also, collect items of interest such as interesting facts, anecdotes, cartoons, up-to-date statistics that might prove useful in supporting your presentation. Notes should be prepared well in advance of the time that the presentation needs to be given to enable you to practice and refine the text.

Prepare your presentation notes, which are different from the written paper that often accompanies an oral presentation. While the latter might be in the form of a full essay or academic paper, your presentation notes should take the form of a list of main points, possibly with some expanded text, to which you will add dialogue during the presentation. Keep in mind that it is possible to prepare a full text that can be read as a speech, but this tends to be lifeless and boring for the audience and it is recommended that this approach be avoided. Remember that a full written paper typically includes more detail than can be covered in a talk. It is necessary for your oral presentation to limit yourself to discussing a few main points only and not attempt to cover all the detail that would be possible in a written paper.

Notes should include memory prompts, such as keywords or phrases which provide you with the main signposts for your talk. Notes can be written on cards that fit into the palm of the hand (palm cards). Ensure that cards or pages are numbered so they can be easily reordered if they become jumbled.

Compose

This is the blood sweat and tears part of the preparation process. You need to get all your facts organized, develop your stories, and develop opening and closing. There is a later chapter on Slideshows, so we will concentrate mostly on developing the content in this section.

The first topic that we will discuss with composition is the structure of the presentation. The structure of the presentation can vary from presenter to presenter and based on style and subject matter. As a presenter, you may feel that you have great points to share, but these points won't be remembered and appreciated until you get the structure of your presentation right. There is another major benefit in using a clear structure for your presentation. The structure helps your audience to know where they are and where they are going. Thus, it addresses the basic human curiosity and gives them reassurance. As the plot of your infotainment progresses, the structure creates tension and gives resolution like a good story. Use an appropriate structure of presentation to make your presentation more memorable.

Organize your material according to some 'organizing principle'. This may be
organizing facts in chronological order, by theme, or in the order of importance. There are some basic structures that are familiar to audiences and that can be adapted to most presentations. We will talk about 7 presentation structures and how and when to use them effectively. The presentation structures are:

1. Five paragraph Essay
2. Day in the life
3. Need - Solution
4. Last Solution Standing
5. Story Structure
6. Chronological Structure
7. Demonstration Structure

The most basic structure is to have an opening, body, and summary. This structure reminds me of my college prep writing course. A technique we learned in the class was the classic five-paragraph essay. The five-paragraph essay is a popular model of composition that consists of five parts such as introduction, three body paragraphs, and conclusion. The foundation of the five-paragraph essay is the formula "thesis + antithesis = synthesis". The main point of this piece of writing is to express a personal author's point of view using true arguments.

So, the Five-Paragraph Essay is the first method to organize your presentation. This is a simple written format but easily adapted to presentations. It is also a format that is familiar and accepted by audiences. The basic outline for a five-paragraph essay is:

1. Introduction. (Interesting information to capture the audience)
2. Body paragraph A. First point. (Details/ Examples/Arguments, etc.)
3. Body paragraph B. Second point. (Details/ Examples/Arguments, etc.)

4. Body paragraph C. Third point. (Details/ Examples/Arguments, etc.)
5. Conclusion (summary of the main ideas)

As each of the five parts has its own specific features, it is better to follow some recommendations to compose the content in a competent and interesting way. These ideas can be used when composing the content of your presentation or for writing an article or memo.

The Introduction is the first part of the five-paragraph essay. An introduction is the opportunity to put your talk into context. You should capture the audience's interest and accomplish a few specific goals here. Try to start with something interesting, you can even use a short story or an anecdote. Never say something like "I am going to tell you about..." It is a boring line. Use your imagination to make people listen to the rest of your presentation with interest. It is important to express your specific point of view and explain the beginning of your work. This is where your main message goes.

The next part is the body that consists of three main arguments or points. The first one should be opened with a transitional sentence to lead the audience into the first piece of evidence you use to support your thesis statement. The second and third parts should follow the same rules. Support your main idea using details and examples. Make sure that every sentence of your five-paragraph presentation proves or reflects your main thesis. Do not forget to check your grammar, spelling, and constructions of the sentences. Try to vary the structures of the sentences and enrich your vocabulary with such word combinations as: by comparison, as a rule, as a result, in fact, moreover, naturally, traditionally, for this reason, surely, yet it follows that, overall, simply put, etc.

The Conclusion is the most difficult paragraph. So, it performs some very significant functions. The conclusion should wrap up the essay and summarize the general points. The Conclusion reminds your readers about the main aspects of your presentation. It is very effective to end your Conclusion with a question or call for action. The strong and well-organized Conclusion can fulfill and resolve your work. You must summarize the main points of your presentation. Do not repeat the specific examples, just restate the Introduction with originality.

The second way to organize material for your presentation is the "Day In The Life" structure. The Day in the Life is a real-life example of one complete circuit through a solution. I present medical software so often I will demonstrate a Day in the Life of a patient. I will show the patient from check-in to check out and the billing and resolution of the claim. This approach is effective because it generates instant familiarity for the audience. It gives the presentation an immediate context. The audience is experiencing that "day in the life" every day.

The third way to organize your presentation is the Need-Solution structure. This technique is best used when you are presenting to persuade an audience. I present in a lot of sales type opportunities, so I use the Need-Solution structure often. Discovery information is important for this approach. You need to know what the problems are to present them to the audience. Begin by framing the need or issue at a high level, in 1 -3 minutes. Then go into the problem in-depth, making both intellectual and emotional arguments for the severity of the problem. This is setting up the tension for the presentation. Assuming an hour-long speech, you should spend 15-20 minutes on the problem. Then, give the solution, including the benefits of it to the audience. This is the resolution for the audience. Finally, give the audience something to do in the end. Give them an action step. Something simple and relevant to the solution.

Next, use the Last Solution Standing method when you are presenting a particularly contentious subject. If the subject has strong supporters on both sides or more than two sides of the issue, then this method is effective. Last Solution Standing is a variant of the Needs-Solution structure. With this method, you frame the problem or issue quickly as an introduction. Then, you explore the issue in more depth. This should be the first third of the presentation. After the deep dive, you tackle the possible solutions of your opponents. Do this in a real and thoughtful way, first presenting the pro side of the solution, and then giving one or two reasons why you think it won't work. Do this for each of the other established positions. Don't just present straw man arguments. Give these positions real credit, as if you believed them. Then, once all the other alternatives are discussed, and the problems with them, give your own solution. Your proposed solution is the one that's left when all the others have been shot down. It's the leftover or the last solution standing.

Method number five is the Classic Story Structure. Use this structure when you have a story to tell. For example, if you are talking about your new company or a new product, and you want to enliven the description with some narrative. Begin by describing the basic situation giving only the relevant detail and introducing the hero (if there is one) in quick brush strokes. Next, introduce a complication – a rival, a new marketplace entrant, and so on. Finally, resolve the crisis that follows from the complication.

The sixth way is the Chronological Structure. Use the Chronological Structure when you've got a history to relate to the audience. What happens next? is the natural response of someone listening to an interesting history. The keyword is 'interesting. I see many presentation structures use Chronological Structure mostly because it is easy. This happened and then this happened, in order. I'm not a big fan of chronological storytelling unless the story itself is compelling and inherently interesting. Otherwise, you want to use the Classic Story Structure. A variant of this method is to begin at the end of something, with a startling result, and then circle back to tell the beginning. Here is how we got to where we are. That's interesting if the stakes are high and everyone is interested in the result. If you were telling the story of Facebook, for example, you might start with the end. Billionaires, fabulous success, and a lawsuit, and then go back to the beginning to see how everyone ended up there. You'd have the plot of the movie The Social Network.

Lastly, use the Demonstration Structure when you've got a product to demonstrate. I think that Steve Jobs did this type of presentation better than almost anyone else. First talk about the why. Why the product is amazing, why it's needed, what problems it solves for people, and so on, and then demo the actual product in all its glory. The exact form the demo takes will, of course, depend on the product, but make sure it works and doesn't get bogged down in the details. Just show it doing something really cool for the audience, and then hint at all the other things it could do. This presentation style needs to be short and quick. It is really a visual Need-Solution structure. You want to show them the reason, show how you fix it and give them the benefit. When you spend a lot of time going through details, this type of presentation can quickly turn into product training. Leave them wanting more.

These seven structures should cover most of the situations in which you find yourself speaking. Each of these structures can be enlivened with brief examples, stories, and factoids along the way. Specificity is the stuff of life in public speaking, but only when used sparingly and to specifically document certain impacts or problems. Too much detail and any good structure immediately become deadly. A presentation is a good way to convey information, to persuade, and to move your audience to action.

Now that we have our structure defined, we can talk specifically about sections of the presentation. Let's start with the opening.

Your first task is getting your audience's attention and to create a connection. It is critical to quickly develop a rapport with the audience. A great way to do this is to relate a personal story, the 'why' of your presentation. Why are you passionate about this topic? How does this topic relate to your life? If you lead in with a personal story, it's much easier for people to relate to your topic. And your personal story

65

establishes authority. To grab your audience's attention, see if you can start in a way that's unexpected.

The introduction or opening enables you to provide the audience with a road map to assist them to follow your discussion as it progresses. In the opening you should:

1. Need a strong beginning
2. Few seconds to convince audience:
    - −I will not waste your time
    - −I am well organized
    - −I know who you are
    - −I know my subject

3. Introduce the problem to be addressed and context
4. State purpose, scope, and the main message
5. Give an outline of the presentation

Now that we have our structure defined and our introduction, you need to lay out exactly how to overcome the pain points to reach the desired outcome. The body of the presentation is the meat and potatoes part of the talk. It is the section in which your arguments are presented and developed. It is critical for the talk to be presented in such a way that the audience can follow it and keep up with it. The presentation should flow smoothly from one point to the next with the links between different points clearly indicated to tell a coherent story. Consider the use of 'signpost' words (e.g. Firstly, As well as, Next, in contrast, However, Finally, etc.) to assist your listeners. This section makes up the bulk of the presentation. As a rule, the Body should make up 75 percent of the presentation time.

The best presentations are conversational. Even if you've worked them out to the letter, they still need to sound spontaneous. The way to write conversationally is to read aloud your draft to others. Whenever you notice that a sentence sounds contrived, mark it for further work. What often works is to shorten sentences, use simple language and use contractions, such as 'you'll' instead of 'you will'. These rehearsals are a key part of building confidence. Once you have laid out how to achieve the desired outcome, it's time for the closing.

In the closure, it's time to talk about how it feels when you achieve the benefits. Maybe you can give examples of others who also achieved success to inspire and motivate. It's a good idea to repeat briefly the main steps of your body of the presentation. In other words, you need to remind them briefly of the main content of your presentation. You should aim to tie the whole talk together. You should summarize and emphasize the main points presented in the body of the talk, develop conclusions, and review any implications. No new ideas should be introduced in the conclusion. Link the Conclusion with the Introduction. Restate the assignment question/topic and show that you have covered all the points that you said in your Introduction you would cover. Use the Conclusion to reinforce your main arguments and to motivate the audience.

Part of the conclusion could be the call to action. You need to outline the next step for your listeners. What should they do now in order to move closer to the desired outcome? Are there special resources they can access? Is there an action they can do today that will start them on the right path?

Things to remember about the conclusion of the presentation are:

1. Must have a clear end to talk
2. A brief and simple summary of the main points
3. Reinforce the main message
4. Call to Action if appropriate

As you can see from the notes above, the key strategy for creating a riveting presentation is to set up dramatic tension, using the structure that sets up a tension between the pain points that the audience experiences and the desired outcomes that your presentation offers. Most importantly, if you use archetypal story threads that bind the parts of the presentation together, you can create a memorable presentation.

Practice

We will go over some general commentary about practice as it pertains to building the presentation here. Please see Chapter 6 on practice for specific practicing techniques.

You have several choices on how to deliver your speech or presentation. Keep these choices in mind as you create it and as you practice it. You want to be able to talk through the presentation, in a well-paced natural tone. Based on your goal with the delivery, practice the appropriate method.

Talk, don't read!

You have several choices for how you deliver your speech	
Memorizing the Speech + allows eye contact - difficult for long speeches - room for precision errors - no room for improvising	**Reading From a Text** + ensures precision - does not sound natural - no room for improvising - hinders eye contact
Winging It + sounds natural - has much room for error	**Speaking From Slides** + insures organization + allows eye contact + allows improvising - some room for error

You must convey sincerity and credibility. There is really no faking this one. You must believe what you say 100%. Your audience will see through it if you are just going through the motions. Practice can make you more comfortable with speaking from the mind, not from notes. This boils down to two factors: knowing your content and taking control of your nerves in order to focus.

Try to practice piece by piece. I've found it very helpful to practice each section of my presentation in pieces. I'll focus on one part at a time and memorize the core elements, run through it till I'm comfortable and then move on to the next piece. Then it's just a matter of stringing the pieces together, which is easier.

While practicing my presentation I've found my comfort zone when I can think of the next one or two sentences while speaking. So, I'm on sentence #5 but my mind is already bringing up sentence #6 and #7. I don't have to think too far ahead but just enough that the transition from to and from each sentence is ultra-smooth and simple. Each sentence triggers a reminder for the next one.

Practice your presentation with hand gestures. If you're giving a presentation with nothing in front of you, like a table or podium, then you need to be aware of what you're doing with your hands. You also need to be aware of what your feet will be doing. So, think about your hand gestures and how they relate to what you're saying. If you plan to move around, pace in sync with your words. The hand gestures and where I'm walking are triggers that cue up what I should be saying. An effective speaker moves the upper body. If you don't have to use a podium, walk across the stage so that you are more "reachable" to each side.

Each presentation usually has a timeframe that you need to adhere to, especially if you invite questions at the end. Make sure you time your rehearsals. Then cut your text so that you spend only 80% of the allotted time, to have some time up your sleeve.

Practice in front of people. If you haven't given a lot of presentations this will feel awkward but it's better to get over those feelings now rather than when you're on stage. Given the opportunity, you should seek expert help with your presentation, but be careful about how you take any advice, especially late in the game.

Rehearse your presentation several times prior to th e actual presentation time.

Ensure that the timing is correct, that you can respond appro priately to the visual prompts in your notes
and that the visual aids work. Practice enables you to refine your talk and reorganize
points or trim the discussion, as needed. It also ensures that you are fully familiar with your material, which will help to improve your presentation skills and build confidence. Ask someone to view your practice session(s) to provide suggestions and advice, and to ask some sample questions for you to practice on. The best way to do this is to ask the people closest to you for their candid assessment. You must give people permission, to be honest. Make it safe and don't be defensive. Otherwise, they will just tell you that you are great, and you will never improve. Instead, you want honest, specific feedback. You don't have to act on every suggestion, but you need to carefully consider every suggestion. You need to also thank people for their feedback and affirm how helpful it is to you. If you do so, people will get bolder about sharing it, which is exactly what you want.

Practice as many times as you must to ensure that y ou can deliver the presentation confidently from your notes. When timing your rehearsals make sure that you fully utilize all the tools that you intend to use during the actual presentation.   Sometimes the tools or visual aid activity can take up a lot more time than anticipated.

Find your comfort zone. All the advice in the world won't help if you can't get comfortable with your preparation, practice techniques and ultimately, the presentation itself. Do whatever makes you feel comfortable. The more comfortable you feel, the more confident you feel, and the better things will go.

Adjust

Based on feedback from practice sessions and your live presentation, adjust. If you do a presentation repeatedly, or parts of the same talk, look at what worked and what didn't and adjust as necessary. In later chapters on Debriefing and Plotting the Presentation, we will go over the adjustments in more detail.

The best time to prepare for the next meeting is right after the last one. You should do this when everything is still fresh in your memory. At the very least, I always try to jot down as many notes as I can. I consider this a sort of personal debriefing session. I ask myself, what worked? What do I want to make sure I do again? What didn't work so well? What do I want to make sure that I don't do again?

I have had many people that I present with do quick debriefing sessions with me right after we get off the stage. If you were a standup comic, you would know what jokes worked and what didn't. You might take the duds out to make room for better material. I learn so much with my debriefing session. Literally down to individual words and tones. I had a salesperson constructively criticize the tone I used on a word in my presentation. The way I said something had a negative effect on the presentation. Because this salesperson was observant and told me, I was able to adjust for the next time.

One person I can count on is my wife, Kristi. I can run ideas past her, and she will always give me honest feedback. She sees things with new eyes and gives me ideas that I had not thought of. Unfortunately, she can't be at every presentation I give. So, I must count on others for feedback.

One major adjustment that you can make is if you think you are losing the audience. If I do a presentation, and I think that the audience "just was not getting it," I go back and look at some things to find out where I was not up to par. Some things that might lose an audience include:

1. The topic is not useful or relevant to them
2. They've heard it all before
3. They're lost
4. They're confused
5. It's too much the same as anything

71

6. It's too long

So, to keep your audience's attention, you just need to make sure these things don't happen and if they do adjust.

First, tell the audience how what you're telling them is relevant to them. At the beginning of your presentation, let your audience know why they should listen to your presentation. Answer their question "What's in it for me?" During your presentation, whenever the relevance of your point is not crystal clear add this phrase "What this means to you...." I have a salesperson that tells the audience in his introduction that there are some key facts in the presentation to watch out for. He will name the main points that we are trying to get across. Then he tells the audience that there will be a quiz at the end of the presentation, so listen for the three things.

Second, tell the audience something new. Tell your audience something they don't know. Take them that extra step beyond their current knowledge. Or if you're having to present information, they're already familiar with, add a novel twist or perspective which will have them think about the topic in a new way.

Thirdly, be organized. When you're listening to a presentation, it's easy to get lost. It's not like reading a report where you can flick backward and forwards and check out where you are. As an audience member, you are at the mercy of the presenter. So, when you're the presenter make it easy on your audience. Be organized and let your audience know the organization of your talk. Use short transition sentences to let your audience know when you're moving from one part of your talk to the next.

Fourth, be clear. If your audience can't follow your explanations, they'll drop out. In a presentation, it's difficult for an audience member to say, "Can you just go back over that bit again?" Practice the complex bits of your presentation on a friend or colleague and get feedback on the clarity of your explanations. Refine your explanations until your practice audience can grasp the explanation immediately.

Fifth, build in variety. Humans notice a change. For example, you don't notice the air conditioning until it turns off. Use this human trait to keep your audience's attention. Here are things you can change throughout your presentation:

1. Where you stand as you present
2. The type of visual aid you're using (slides, flipchart, whiteboard, nothing)
3. Type of content (facts, opinions, story, statistics, metaphors)
4. Style of content (emotional, logical)
5. Delivery method (you are talking, discussion, Q&A)
6. What the audience is doing (listening to you, writing something down, talking with their neighbor, asking you questions)

Lastly, make it short. Sitting passively for any length of time is difficult. A stand-alone presentation should be no longer than 60 minutes. In a day-long training session, I make sure that I'm not talking for more than 10-15 minutes at a time, without the audience doing something.

When creating your presentation here are 10 commandments to follow to get you through.

I.	VI.
Thou shalt be neat	*Thou shalt use color*
II.	VII.
Thou shalt be clear	*Thou shalt illustrate*
III.	VIII.
Thou shalt covet brevity	*Thou shalt make eye contact*
IV.	IX.
Thou shalt not cover thy naked slides	*Thou shalt skip slides in a long talk*
V.	X.
Thou shalt write large	*Thou shalt practice*

Script Writing, Outlining and Storyboarding

I am a big fan of scriptwriting and the process of writing your presentation script has many benefits. I am not a fan of script reading. I use the script as a preparation process and to document my presentation to use for other purposes.

The first benefit of scriptwriting is to get the presentation out of your head. If I have a presentation idea rattling around in my noggin, once I commit it to paper or word processor that idea becomes more real for me. I can start to work with the idea and manipulate and organize it. I can build my messaging and supporting points. Just getting the idea into another medium forces me to think about the idea enough to talk, type or write it down.

When I write a script, I record not only what I will say, but what actions I will take. I put where I navigate in my system and where to click in the script. This lets me think through the process and match the process to the client or prospect. I will run through the script several times when I practice a scripted presentation. It usually takes me three practices with a script to eliminate the need to use the script.

The script lets you write everything out and start massaging the words the way you want. It also gives you a benchmark against which you can practice and refine things.

As you develop your script, another organization technique that I use is dividing up my material. I divide the content of my presentation into categories and then color code the categories. For example, I put my facts and figures and more lecture content in black, case studies and return on investment in green, stories in blue, etc. Then I can look at the script and see if the presentation has too much of one type of style or color. This lets me make sure the presentation is well balanced between facts, and stories and studies. I can be confident with the balance of my presentation before giving it.

One technique that I have learned is to script my opening and closing remarks. I am generally at ease in front of an audience, but I don't want to leave that to chance. My opening remarks are scripted and written down just in case I am nervous at first. I can get into my rhythm by starting to read. I very rarely use the script, and if I do, I will only need to read a few words. I do feel more secure just knowing that the script is there.

I do the same scripting method for my closing remarks. If I do a formalized question and answers session, I will put my closing thoughts right after. Having the scripted closing remarks creates a situation where you have prepared and practiced the last words that the audience will hear from you.

Sometimes I do presentations where a script is provided. When this happens, it is like an instant discovery visit. The information that the group is interested in seeing is almost always included in the script. It normally takes me longer to prepare for a script that I did not write. Often, I will rearrange the script into my own flow. I will still cover all the items, in a different order. In my industry, often there is a consultant involved that provides a script for a presentation or demonstration.

Outlines

Outlines are my go-to preparation tool. Outlines allow you to quickly organize your thoughts and assemble related information. I have been outlining ever since I wrote papers in grade school. Whenever I have a new presentation, the outline is the first thing that I complete. I sometimes do write paper outlines on my legal pad. I also use products like PowerPoint to do an outline. When you use tools like PowerPoint, the outline can be recycled to create the slide show itself.

When I decided to write this book, the first thing I created was a basic outline. For presentations, I will list all my main topics and then the points that I want to talk about beneath each main idea. I will normally do a brainstorming outline, which will become a working document, where I will add, move, and delete elements as the process of creating the presentation progresses. When the outline is finished, I have the skeleton of the presentation that I can use for developing my graphics and bullet points.

Storyboarding

Going beyond the outline is the storyboard. Storyboarding was pioneered by filmmakers and animators. We can use the same concepts in the development of other forms of storytelling, including presentations. The storyboarding process allows you to flesh out themes and look for patterns as you create your context.

Instead of a text outline, storyboarding is a way to visualize the story of your context. Walt Disney developed the use of storyboards in the 1920s, allowing filmmakers to see a blueprint of the movie before going into production. You tack your ideas, in the picture and/or short text form, upon the wall, so you can see the entire sequence and continuity of ideas.

The drawings do not have to be pretty, but they need to convey the meaning and feeling behind the idea. A good storyboarder is a good storyteller and a good pitchman. The storyboard pitch is one of the great performance arts developed in the 20th Century, yet no one ever gets to see it. It happens behind the scenes before the movie is even made. I have seen special features on DVDs from Pixar that show some of the storyboarding sessions. They are fascinating. The storyboarding sessions are really a sales pitch with visuals (drawings). This makes storyboarding a perfect technique to study for presenting.

Walt Disney used to say, "At our studio, we don't write stories, we draw them."

With storyboarding you can tell the story or the pitch of the presentation, in a simple form, before spending time on any details. Storyboards allow you to see what points work and don't work in the context of your story and can save a lot of unnecessary work. Think of it as your presentation in panels like in a comic book. You can use storyboarding to pitch a presentation internally or help develop the presentation itself.

I have seen people make storyboards using sheets of paper tacked or taped to a wall. I have seen groups use whiteboards. My old favorite method was to use Post-It Notes. Post-Its are small, to keep your ideas simple and they are already sticky. My new favorite is the collapsible dry erase panels that we talked about in the gear section.

STAGING

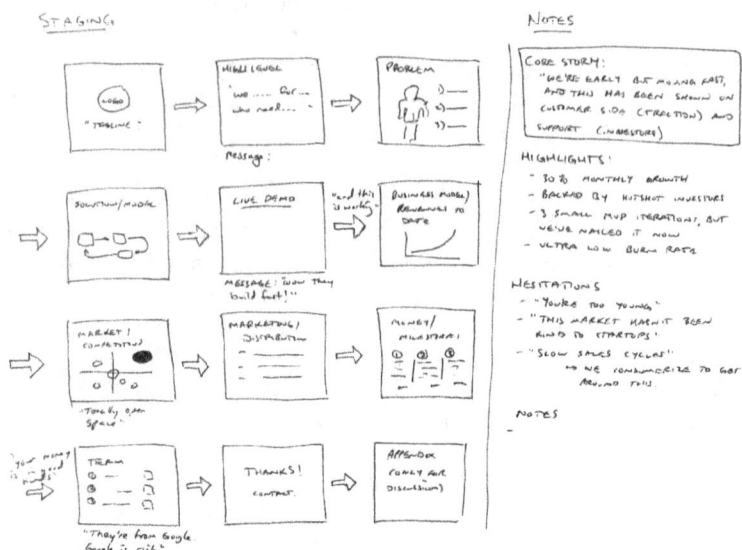

CORE STORY:
"WE'RE EARLY BUT MOVING FAST,
AND THIS HAS BEEN SHOWN ON
CUSTOMER SIDE (TRACTION) AND
SUPPORT (INVESTORS)"

HIGHLIGHTS:
- 30% MONTHLY GROWTH
- BACKED BY HOTSHOT INVESTORS
- 3 SMALL MVP ITERATIONS, BUT
  WE'VE NAILED IT NOW
- ULTRA LOW BURN RATE

HESITATIONS
- "YOU'RE TOO YOUNG"
- "THIS MARKET HASN'T BEEN
  KIND TO STARTUPS"
- "SLOW SALES CYCLES"
     ↳ WE CONSUMERIZE TO GET
       AROUND THIS

NOTES

78

Chapter 5: Use of Slide Show Presentation Software

"Create slides that demonstrate, with emotional proof, that what you're saying is true not just accurate."

Seth Godin

This is not a how-to book about how to use presentation software, so I will just point out give some basic slideshow rules as it pertains to presentations. I am going to assume that you already use or have used slideshow software. If that is not the case, I suggest going through the tutorial included with the software to make yourself familiar with it. There are also lots of online resources to help you. I have used PowerPoint as my go-to slide presentation software for many years. The techniques that we discuss, however, are not PowerPoint specific.

Back in my debate days, we organized everything on index cards. We would spend hours finding facts and figures and other evidence and cutting and pasting the snippets onto 3x5 cards. When it was time to give your speech in the debate, you would take your cards and organize them in the order that you wanted to present. You would get up and make your argument and use your cards to back up your position. I have always thought of a slideshow, or presentation software as my electronic pack of index cards. I can still put my points on the cards plus my evidence and impacts. I can rearrange the slides based on facts that I find out about the presentation. I can reuse slides and borrow slides from other decks.

The first thing that I use the presentation software for is organizing and planning my presentation. The presentation software is a great tool for outlining even if you never project that version of the presentation on the screen. I start out giving each of the main topics of the presentation its own slide. Then I will put my points for each topic underneath. A simple example would be:

I. Topic A

    Point 1

        Fact a

        Fact b

    Point 2

        Fact a

        Fact b

Here is a quick slideshow template for you. If you are an early user of presentation software, you can create a template like this and use it as your starting point for future presentations.

Slide 1: My Presentation Title

Slide 2: My Message

Slide 3: Topic 1

Slide 4: Topic 1 Evidence/Data/Info Slide

Slide 5: Topic 1 Story/Impact

Slide 6: Topic 2

Slide 7: Topic 2 Evidence/Data/Info Slide

Slide 8: Topic 2 Story/Impact

Slide 9: Topic 3

Slide 10: Topic 3 Evidence/Data/Info Slide

Slide 11: Topic 3 Story/Impact

Slide 12: My Message (restated and summarized)

Slide 13: My Presentation Title

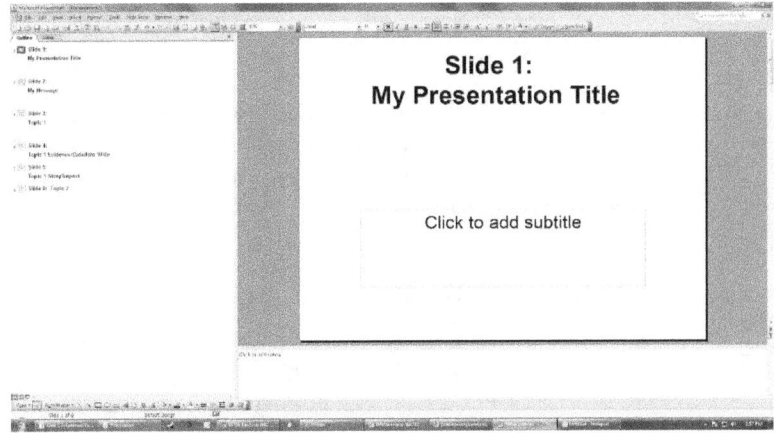

So, in thirteen slides you have a basic outline that will work for any kind of presentation. This will help you next time you get the "Oh no, where do I start feeling." You can, of course, add more topics and data slides, etc. There is no strict rule on how many slides, you should have. You need enough slides to cover the points that you are trying to get across.

Rules for Slideshow success

1. Use the slideshow to help, not confuse the audience. What the audience sees must match what the audience hears. Journalism school professors preach "Get the words down first, then match the pictures to them." Each slide should reinforce the words coming out of your mouth. Everybody loses when words and pictures on the screen don't match the audio. I have heard executives say, "The audience can read all those additional facts while they listen to the speaker." They can't... it gives the audience a headache. The presentation becomes too much work. You lose your entertainment value. You lose the audience's attention and retention.

2. Text on the slides should be interesting with as few words as possible and in as big a font as possible. I have seen all kinds of guidelines for fonts and text size and the

number of words per slide. I am not going to give you hard and fast rules here.

First, you need to make sure the words on the screen support the words spoken by the presenter. The words do not have to be exact, but they need to have the same meaning.

Next, make sure the words on the slide can be read easily from the back of the room. Project the presentation in the room you are presenting in and walk to the back of the room. Can you read the slide? If not, increase the font or lessen the number of words on the slide, or both.

I see all the time where a presenter references an article in their talk. The presenter navigates to the next slide, and they have cut and pasted the article into the slideshow. Every time the presenter will say something like "Sorry you won't be able to read this but..." Don't do this. If the audience can't see it, what is the point of putting it in the slideshow? It will turn the audience's attention off or at least down a notch. The better technique is to put some keywords from the article in the slideshow. Or put a reference in the slide show like:

Article Name

Wall Street Journal, April 5, 2013

The Lessons of Zombie-Mania

The Lessons of
Zombie-Mania

Article
Wall Street Journal
April 5, 2013

http://online.wsj.com/article/
SB10001424127887323611604578398952000653448.html

Then you can use the actual article as a handout or give the audience the link to go and read the article.

Lastly, when you are creating your sides use a few memorable strong words out of the text that you are speaking. When the audience reads and hears the same idea their retention is increased. We are trying to keep the audience's attention.

5 problems to watch out for

1. No point to the presentation

2. No benefit for the audience

3. No flow

4. Too detailed

5. Too long

I did a presentation in New York for a network of physicians. I had a director level person in charge of giving a corporate overview and I was responsible for the product demonstration. A total of three hours was allocated for the entire presentation. The Director started doing his presentation slide show and did not finish until two and a half hours later. He had 170 slides in his slideshow. He didn't even get to them all. The audience was exhausted. This was absolute "Death by Slideshow."

"Oh no! Not another PowerPoint Presentation" This reaction is not unique. When talking to people in my seminars and social settings, the message I get is clear. Audiences are tired of worn-out PowerPoint presentations! Does this mean we should jettison this technology and go back to the "stone age", in giving our presentations? No more than we should ban television because of the likes of Jerry Springer and Temptation Island. The medium itself is not to blame, it is how that medium is used that falls short.

Very often, presenters rely solely on their slideshow software to provide every bit of their presentation's creativity. The problem with this approach is that the entertainment value of slideshow programs leaves a lot to be desired. When a speaker uses the software as a crutch, instead of as an enhancement tool, it can give a presenter a false sense of security about a bad presentation. Being a presenter, I am extra critical of presentations. I've sat through many a bad presentation where the insecure presenter just hides behind a barrage of screen activity, using every transition and effect as a gimmick, rather than having good structure and story in making their points.

So, how should this medium be best used? Obviously, there are millions of reasons for a presentation, and therefore, millions of effective and creative ways to deliver it. Creativity can take several forms, from the spontaneous quip to the extravagant special effects of a Hollywood blockbuster. Keep in mind, though, that a crummy movie with very impressive special effects is still a crummy movie, and the same rule applies to presentations. Things that may work well in some presentations will not do so in others. Next, we will talk about some general guidelines for the successful use of electronic slides.

First, you want to add, not detract from the content of the presentation. The slides should enhance your talk, not compete with it. If you find your presentation including phrases like "Here is a picture of how we envision the solution working in your environment", or "Here is how the process works after implementation,", along with the appropriate slides, then the slideshow is probably working to your advantage. If, on the other hand, we interrupt our thought flow, and that of our audience, to draw attention, there is probably something lacking in the content. In one notable presentation I attended, the presenter (who must have just learned a bunch of new PowerPoint tricks) proceeded to present with every transition, effect, sound, build, bullet, clip art, and color that PowerPoint had to offer. There were multiple effects and formats on every slide. The presenter was very proud of himself and laughed out loud at the 'Vroom Vroom' sound effect and the cheesy clipart Corvette car zooming across the screen. The audience was overwhelmed and basically horrified. The purpose of the presentation was lost. The salesperson had told me before the presentation that he had created an updated slideshow. My mistake was trusting him and not looking at the presentation first.   The intended effect had failed, and the audience was focused on all the affects that flashed in front of them instead of the point of the talk.

Secondly, you need to know your topic. By using presentation programs as a supplement to, rather than the substance of an effective presentation, you insure yourself against the unexpected failure of almost any part of the presentation. During a seminar on software security, with a room full of attendees, my slides stopped projecting from the laptop to the screen. After a little joke, and a couple of shadow puppets with the white light coming out of the projector, (you must do at least one shadow puppet, right?) I continued for over fifteen minutes on the topic I was covering. Since I no longer had to be up in front of the room, this gave me the opportunity to wander out away from my laptop and into the group, which I love to do. Not only did the absence of slides not ruin the seminar, but it also enhanced it, because it gave the audience and me a shared humorous experience that I referred to a few times for humorous effect. I kept teasing someone in the front row about being the person who had unplugged the video cable earlier. This could not have been possible, had the visual part of the presentation been its main support.

Third, know your medium. If something goes wrong with the equipment or presentation, you should have a good feel for how everything works. I recently watched a presenter delivering a talk, accidentally stop the slide presentation and couldn't get it going again. The program had not closed, just gone from "slide view" to "slide creation view" and simply had to be restarted by clicking a button on the screen. By not knowing how to do this simple step, the presenter ruined their credibility and wound up looking sheepishly on as a member of her staff came up to the podium and restarted her presentation. This is an extreme example, but it also pays to not only know how to run the program itself, but how to diagnose other technical problems that may occur.

In the presentation to which I referred above, where the image from my laptop suddenly stopped showing on the screen, it was helpful to know a bit about the equipment. During the short break that I called after the outage, I was able to diagnose that a member of the audience had accidentally kicked the video cable, dislodging it slightly from my projector. (It was not the audience member that I had been teasing). While I am not an expert on every type of projector on the market, nor would I want to be, I knew enough about the workings of the system, in general, to fix the problem within minutes, rather than waiting helplessly for the hotel media staff.

Fourth, the most notorious misuse of presentation programs is putting everything on the screen that you intend to say and reading from the slide. Please take my advice, if your presentation contains all the words you are going to say, stay home and e-mail them to your audience where they can read them at their leisure. Slides should be reserved for visuals that add to the presentation, diagrams, or information that the audience can take special notes on. In fact, slides can be used effectively in hundreds of ways. I saw one presenter who said something like, "Here are a few of the laws that govern the operation of a small business today". He then proceeded to show several slides of laws, rules, and regulations that increasingly got smaller and smaller in type size and more rapid in succession. The point was well made that there was a good reason to have a good business attorney.

One way that the slides should not be used is as a script to read from. Even bullet points are a bit suspect. If the slides have nothing to add to the presentation other than being a guide for you to follow, leave them off. In the technical training field, there are many folks who, because they have some technical knowledge, assume that they are effective presenters because they can read from slides. We call such people slide-readers. They can always be counted on to put the audience promptly to sleep. They fail at communication by using the slides as a crutch, rather than an enhancement. Slide-readers never make a connection to the audience. Attendees can read the slides themselves; they do not need the slides to read to them. Slide-readers have done more to damage the viability of technical presentations than cold coffee.

Your success in delivering an effective, memorable presentation can be greatly enhanced with presentation software. It will, however, rarely come from integrating new plug-ins, images or Flash content, or by fielding dozens of slides that contain the verbiage of your entire presentation. Used wisely, creative elements and bullet slides have their time and place, but the art of communication involves a much more expansive universe of interaction. The bottom line is that the purpose of a presentation isn't to fine-tune your graphics until they look great, or to display all your ideas from a screen. The object of an effective presentation is to communicate important ideas and messages. Using presentation programs should add to, and not detract from, that goal.

Slide show presentations, whether they are made with PowerPoint or other applications, are a great way to support a speech, and help the audience visualize complicated concepts or focus attention on a subject. However, a bad slideshow presentation can achieve the opposite of your goal. Badly designed slides with too much text or bad graphics can distract or worse, irritate the audience. In the next part of the chapter, we will go over some tips that will help you create presentations with a professional look and concise content, avoiding the most common mistakes.

I am extra critical when I watch others present, but I have been tempted to chew off an arm to escape some mind-numbing slide shows. It is usually bad design and flawed delivery that is to blame. Many of the Slideshow presentations I am forced to sit through seem to combine all the world's worst presentation habits into one unbearable hour of pain, sadness, and cheesy fonts. Next let's discuss some things I have learned from years of delivering slideshow presentations and watching others deliver slideshow presentations, including format and design, colors, fonts, images, and charts.

Remember that your slides are only there to support, not to replace your talk. You'll want to tell a story, describe your data or explain circumstances, and only provide keywords through your slides. If you read your slides and if you do it slowly and badly, the audience will get bored and stop listening. If you lose the attention of your audience, everything will be lost. It won't matter how ingenious your design is or how brilliantly you picked colors and keywords.

Design and Text

Your audience defines the content of your presentation. Your presentation is for the benefit of the audience but boring an audience with bullet point after bullet point is of little benefit to them. When designing your slides here are some items help you keep your audience in mind:

1. What do they know?

2. What do you need to tell them?

3. What do they expect?

4. What will be interesting to them?

5. What can you teach them?

6. What will keep them focused?

7. Answer these questions and boil your slides down to the very essentials.

Organizing your slides is an essential part of creating your slide show presentation. I have an archive of my past presentations. Often, I will take bits and pieces of old presentations and incorporate those ideas from the old slideshow into the new presentation when appropriate. When organizing your slides construct your presentation in a clear and logical way. Remember our presentation types from the Compose Section of the previous chapter. Use a beginning (title slide, introduction); a middle (informational slides); and an end (summary/conclusion). If you use PowerPoint, there is an AutoContent Wizard that can help you structure the show if you get stuck.

Does the presentation fulfill the objective that you set out? Does the presentation convey the necessary message/information? Is it suitable for the target audience? These objectives are going to come from your information that is gathered during discovery.

Is the content clear and focused on the objectives? Does each point lead logically to the next? Is every slide pulling its weight or would the presentation be tighter if you ditched a slide here and there?

How about some supporting and/or ancillary information? In my presentations, I usually include hidden slides that I can jump to if I need to fill time, answer questions, or amplify certain points. Great examples of these types of hidden slides are case studies. I may be trying to make a point, and due to a question, a case study from the archive might be appropriate. I can just into the slide sorter and pull up the applicable case study that will give me the intended impact. Most of my presentations will have fifty percent more slides in them than I will actually show.

Now that we have our slides all organized, let's talk about some design elements. As a rule, slides should be consistent in format and appearance but not boring. Keep slides simple, neat and uncluttered, with space around the margins to ensure that the whole slide can be projected.

Here are some quick rules for your slide design and composition:

1. Don't copy & paste slides from different sources.

2. Keep the design very basic and simple. It shall not distract.

3. Pick an easy-to-read font face.

4. Carefully select font sizes for headers and text.

5. Leave room for highlights, such as images or take-home messages.

6. Decorate scarcely but well.

7. Don't ever let the design restrict your message.

8. Consistently use the same font face and sizes on all slides.

9. Match colors.

10. Layout continuity from frame to frame conveys a sense of completeness

11. Headings, subheadings, and logos should show up in the same spot on each frame

12. Margins, fonts, font size, and colors should be consistent

13. Graphics should be located in the same general position on each frame

14. Lines, boxes, borders, and open space also should be consistent throughout

As far as formatting goes, the most important rule is consistency. You clearly need a consistent visual theme throughout your presentation. Have you used the same fonts and formats for common elements (titles, text boxes, bulleted lists, drawing objects) across all slides? Are the case and punctuation consistent? Have you applied a theme or background style to all the slides (or used a template) to create a unified design for the presentation?

Most templates included in slideshow software have been seen by your audience countless times. Your audience expects a unique presentation with new (at least to them) content. Otherwise, why would they be attending your talk? No audience will be excited about a cookie-cutter presentation, and we must, therefore, shy away from any supporting visuals, such as the ubiquitous PowerPoint Design Template, that suggests your presentation is formulaic or prepackaged.

You can make your own background templates, which will be more tailored to your needs. You can then save the PowerPoint file as a Design Template (.pot) and the new template will appear among your standard Microsoft templates for your future use. You can also purchase professional templates online. I generally make my own backgrounds. I use a graphic that is applicable to my presentation, and then use effects in a graphics tool to fade it into the background. You end up with the essence of the picture without being distracted by the presentation.

Your slides should have plenty of white space or negative space. Do not feel compelled to fill empty areas on your slide with your logo or other unnecessary graphics or text boxes that do not contribute to better understanding.

The less clutter you have on your slide, the more powerful your visual message will become. I had a problem with white space myself for a long time. My tendency was to fill up any available empty space with logos or something. It took me a long time to clean up my slides.

Which brings us to the issue of text. PowerPoint is NOT a word processor!
The point of a PowerPoint slide is not to cram as much information into a single slide as possible. The idea of a slide is to have memory joggers that trigger thinking in the audience. The slides are there to enhance your overall presentation, not to replace you. If it takes more than a few seconds to process the text on any given slide, it's too much. That means you do not need to even have complete sentences. Simple statements work just fine. If a busy slide doesn't overwhelm your audience, it will most certainly distract them. Instead of listening to you, they'll read ahead.

Once you have a rough draft of your presentation, review it with the following goals in mind:

1. Replace complete sentences with keywords and phrases

2. Get rid of unnecessary clip art

3. Remove punctuation

By following these steps, you may reduce content by as much as half, and your presentation will be more focused.

Far too many presenters stand on stage reading the slides. It turns out that most of the audience members probably are literate and can read the slides for themselves. The purpose of a presentation is not to read the presentation for them. A presentation is about explaining things to people that go above and beyond what they get in the slides. If it weren't, you might as well just send them your slides.

The best slides may have no text at all. This may sound insane given the dependency of text slides today, but the best slides will be virtually meaningless without the narration (that is you). Remember, the slides are meant to support the narration of the speaker, not make the speaker unnecessary.

Many people often say something like, "Sorry I missed your presentation. I hear it was great. Can you just send me your slides?" But if they are good slides, they will be of little use without you. Instead of a copy of your presentation slides, it is far better to prepare a written document that highlights your content from the presentation and expands on that content. Audiences are much better served to receive a detailed, written handout as a takeaway from the presentation, rather than a mere copy of your slides. If you have a detailed handout or publication for the audience to be passed out after your talk, you need not feel compelled to fill your PowerPoint slides with a great deal of text.

Now that you have slides organized and designed, you can define how slides act and move from one to the other. Use object builds and slide transitions judiciously. Object builds (also called animations), such as bullet points, should not be animated on every slide. Some animation is a good thing but sticks to the most subtle and professional (similar to what you might see on the evening TV news broadcast). A simple Left-to-Right Wipe is good for a bullet point. A Move or Fly, for example, is too tedious and slow. I still see them used in many presentations today. Listeners will get bored quickly if they are asked to endure slide after slide of animation. I will use object builds to highlight the point that I am currently talking about. If I have three bulleted statements on the screen, I will have the statements come into view one at a time, so the audience is not distracted by reading ahead.

For transitions between slides, use no more than two or three types of transition effects. Make the transitions simple ones. No swirling transitions with sound effects. Do not place transition effects between all slides. Make the transitions a natural part of the presentation. If you have multiple slides on each topic, use a transition between topics to indicate that you are moving on.

In your template design, if you embed video or links to content on the Internet or a network share, please test it before you walk into a conference room and try presenting it to a dozen people. I can't tell you how frequently I encounter presenters who don't know how to launch an external link from within their slideshow deck or who have linked to an obsolete version of the document they wanted to show. Do your homework and test your links before presenting them.

Many slideshow programs have speaker's notes. During your design, you can prepare some notes that will help you remember what you want to say. If you put your key ideas and facts into the speaker's notes pane, you can refer to them during the show. It is much more professional to glance at your laptop to refer to notes than it is to turn around and read the text from the screen. I have seen speakers use the speakers' notes basically as a teleprompter.

The last item to talk about the design and text front is accuracy. Have you checked to spell, verified names, and tested any links you've included on your slides? This sounds like common sense, but I am astonished at how many times I watch presentations that contain errors. Limiting your text on your design means less chance of misspelling that text. I did a presentation recently at a medical practice. The salesperson started the presentation with a slide showing the prospect's needs that were gathered during discovery. On the discovery slide were three misspelled words. Yikes! An audience member noticed the errors and actually said, out loud, "I guess your solution does not include a spell checker." Do you see what happened? The attendee reflected that error on the slideshow, to our solution.

Color

As part of the design of your slides, your color is something that needs careful consideration. Color is emotional and it evokes feelings and memories. The right color can help persuade and motivate. Studies show that color usage can increase interest and improve learning comprehension and retention. A poor choice of colors can detract from a presentation.

You do not need to be an expert in color theory, but it's good for business professionals to know at least a bit about the subject. Colors can be divided into two general categories: cool (such as blue and green) and warm (such as orange and red). Cool colors work best for backgrounds, as they appear to recede away from us into the background. Warm colors generally work best for objects in the foreground (such as text) because they appear to be coming at us. Reds and oranges are high-energy but can be difficult to stay focused on. Greens, blues, and browns are mellower, but not as attention-grabbing.

It is no surprise, then, that the most ubiquitous PowerPoint slide color scheme includes a blue background with yellow text. Blue and yellow are also complimentary colors on the color wheel, which explains why they work together. You do not need to feel compelled to use this color scheme, although you may choose to use a variation of those colors.

Look at the color wheel below. Colors separated by another color are contrasting colors, also called complementary colors. Adjacent colors harmonize with one another, like Green and Yellow. Colors directly opposite one another are said to clash. Clashing colors provide readability. Good examples are Orange on Blue or Yellow on Blue.

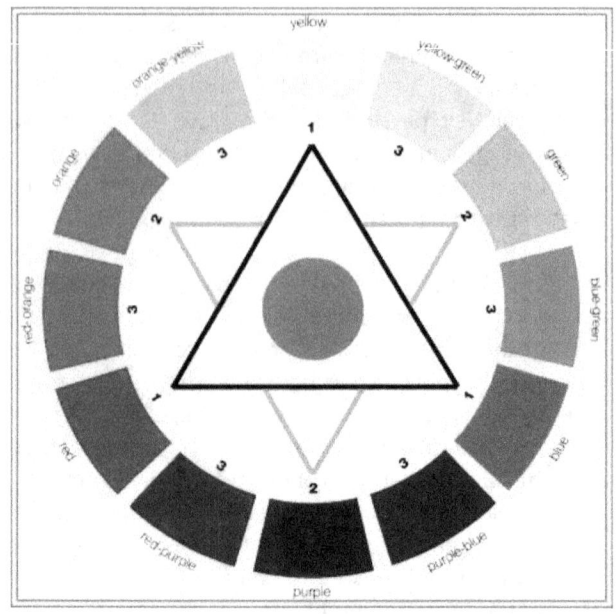

If you are presenting in a dark room (such as a large hall), a dark background (dark blue, gray, etc.) with white or light text will work fine. But if you plan to keep most of the lights on, a light background with black or dark text works much better. In rooms with a good deal of ambient light, a screen image with a dark background and light text tends to washout, but the dark text on a light background will maintain its visual intensity a bit better. White on a dark background should not be used if the audience is more than 20 ft away. In large hall events, avoid white backgrounds. The white screen can be blinding in a dark room. Dark slides with light-colored text work best

Be conscious of people with disabilities. Most disabilities do not interfere with a presentation; however, some do. For instance, red text on a blue background is impossible to see for people who are colorblind, since it won't stop moving. Red text on black has the same effect, and red text on green simply disappears for some people.

Fonts

Choose your fonts well. Fonts communicate subtle messages in and of themselves, which is why you should choose fonts deliberately. Use the same font set throughout your entire slide presentation and use no more than two complementary fonts (e.g., Arial and Arial Bold). Here are some guidelines to help you use fonts effectively in your next presentation. By selecting and using fonts effectively on your presentation slides, you can increase the impact of your message.

How do you decide what fonts to use? Just as you would make choices about any part of your presentation, to choose the best fonts you need to start by considering your message and your audience.

Should your presentation feel formal or informal to your audience? This is a two-part decision. First, you need to decide if the content is formal, such as the accounting numbers for a corporation, or informal, such as the results of a sales contest. Next, consider who you are talking to. Upper management will receive your content better if you use a more formal font rather than something fun and silly. If you're presenting to a group of kids or a weekend retreat, you can go a little wilder with the look of the fonts.

There are three basic categories of fonts: Serif, Sans-Serif, and Script. Here is a description of each font category, some examples of each, when you should use them, and how they affect your presentation.

A serif font is one that has serifs or extra tails at the end of each letter. The most popular serif font is Times Roman, others include Bookman, Century, Garamond, Lucida and Palatino. Serif fonts were designed to be used in documents filled with lots of text. They are printed fonts. I always associate these fonts with newspapers and books. Serif fonts are easier to read at small point sizes, but for onscreen presentations, the serifs tend to get lost due to the relatively low resolution of projectors. If you chose to use a serif font, only use if for a title font where the text will be larger.

A sans-serif font does not the serifs or extra pieces at the ends of the letters. The most popular sans-serif font is Arial, others include Calibri, Century Gothic, Helvetica, Lucida Sans, Tahoma, and Verdana. A sans-serif font is easier to read, so it is best used for either title or body text on a slide so that the viewer can quickly read the point and return their attention to the speaker. Sans- serif fonts are generally best for slideshow presentations and can be read more clearly from farther away. I often choose to use Gill Sans, as it is somewhere in between a serif and a sans-serif font and is professional yet friendly and "conversational." Sans-serif fonts are generally considered less formal.

The third category of fonts is script. A script font is one that tries to emulate handwriting. Some script fonts are Brush Script, Edwardian Script, Freestyle Script, French Script, Papyrus and Vivaldi. A script font is quite hard to read and should not usually be used on a slide since the viewer will spend too much time trying to read the words and not be able to focus on the message.

Once you know what kinds of fonts you want to use, it's time to pick the actual fonts. Because Slideshow software generally comes with a wide variety of fonts, you don't have to stick with just Times New Roman or Arial. You do have to pick the three or four fonts that you want to use in your presentation and stick to them. Map a font to each content type and stick with it. Fonts, like colors, should be used to trigger a reaction or thought from your presentation. By sticking to just a few fonts, you make it easier for your audience to catch clues on what you are sharing. I usually select three fonts, one for my content, one for my titles, and one to grab the audience's attention.

Your first font choice should be the main content font, which you will use for most of your presentation's text. This is the font you will use for your bullet points, for example, and if you are presenting charts and graphics, this is the font you will use to explain or comment on the slide elements. I like to stick with a plain sans-serif font for my main content font, but I don't like to use Helvetica, and Arial because they are so overused. Instead, I use a font like Gill Sans, Calibri, Century Gothic, Helvetica, Lucida Sans, Tahoma, and Verdana. Each of these choices scales well, each is available on most machines, and each has a slightly different feel.

The next choice is for titles, labels, and captions. This font should be a little less formal than the content font, but still very readable at all font sizes. Because you will be using it for both large text (titles) and small text (labels), it is a good idea to check the font out in both sizes before you choose.

Your last font choice is the font that you use to grab the audience's attention. It should fit with the other fonts in the presentation but stand out enough that the audience knows that something important is about to happen. To choose wisely, pick an attention font that is either on every system or that can be easily shared. With the wide variety of fonts out there, this is where you can have fun. Practice matching the attention font to the content. Attention font choices are very personal. I don't have much advice for you on choosing one. All I suggest is to pick the ones upfront that you want to use and stick with them. Sometimes I will just use a bolder bigger version of my content font as my attention font.

Now that you know which fonts you are going to use, you need to decide what size the text should be. The basic answer is, big enough to be seen by the entire audience. Whether you are presenting live to a group of a thousand or creating a kiosk to be run one person at a time, using fonts that are too small is one of the easiest traps you can fall into. The font size is going to depend on the size of the screen and the size of the room.

If you are giving a presentation using a projection system, regular slide text should never be smaller than a sixteen-point character. I try never to go smaller than eighteen points, but I know that isn't always possible. Labels and captions should never be smaller than fourteen points, and bigger is better. Labels on charts don't do much good if they can't be read.

While the fonts and colors you choose have a definite impact on legibility, the single biggest factor is text size. The 8H rule is the time-honored way to make sure that even the folks in the back row can read the text on your slides. The 8H rule says that the maximum viewing distance shouldn't be more than 8 times the height (H) of the screen. If that condition is met then as long as your text is at least 1/25th the height of the screen, then it'll be legible at the maximum viewing distance. That assumes that the person in the back row has good eyes, that the projected image is in focus. This is a minimum, not a recommended size. I have seen this type of rule everywhere from 1.5H to 8H, so there is no agreement on the proper formula.

Based on my research, I created a table that explains if the font size you have selected will be big enough for the room and screen you are using. My table is based on a 6H rule. To use the table, locate the row that corresponds to the height of the screen you are using. Then locate the column that matches the smallest font used on your slides. The intersection of the row and column is the maximum distance that an audience member should be able to easily read the text. For example, if you have 32-point text on your slides and you have a 60-inch screen, the farthest that someone should be from the screen is 46 feet.

Font Size (In Points)

		18	24	28	32	36	40	44
	36	15	22	25	27	30	34	37
	48	20	29	33	37	41	45	49
Screen Height	60	26	35	41	46	51	56	61
(In inches)	72	30	42	49	55	61	67	74

84	35	50	57	64	71	78	86
96	41	57	65	74	82	90	98
120	51	71	82	91	102	112	122
132	56	78	90	101	111	123	134

Even with this information, when I do presentations after my projector is all set up, I will walk to the back of the room to make sure I can read the screen. That is a great way to literally eyeball it.

Keep in mind that if your screen or your distance does not fit into the 8H rule, you'll have to compensate. For example, if the screen is 5 feet high in an 80-foot-deep room, it's only half the recommended size, so you'll need to double the minimum text height to compensate.

While that is the full and correct answer, I know you'd like a simple answer that will work with most room situations. Here are some guidelines for font sizes that will almost always work well:

Title Font – between 36 and 44 points
Body Font – between 24 and 32 points

Choosing attributes on your fonts is something that I use sparingly. Attributes are the little extras that you add to characters to make them stand out without changing their size. The common attributes are bold, italic, underline, shadows, all caps, word art, and highlighting. Like display fonts, they lose their punch when used too much.

Bold makes the lines of the font thicker. It is not always easy to tell bold from regular weight fonts when the presentation is projected. If you use bold, try projecting to see how it turned out. If you find yourself making more than a few words bold on a single slide, it is time to rewrite the text on the slide. Active words need emphasis less than passive ones do, so the more active you can make your text, the better it will be.

Italic slants the tops of the letters of the font to the right. An italic font is harder to read, so it should be used sparingly to emphasize words. The italic for many common fonts does not upsize well. It becomes hard to read very quickly. If you are using italic for emphasis, don't. If you are using it to show motion, consider using animation instead. About the only place I like italic in a presentation is for attribution of a quote or statistic.

Underline is the next attribute on the list. I don't underline much in my presentations. If text is underlined in today's presentations, it means that the text is a link to somewhere else or to the activation of another element. Some people also still use underline for book titles. If you don't mean the text to fall into one of those two buckets, don't underline it.

Shadows place a dark gray shadow of each letter behind the letter slightly to the right and slightly below the letter. A shadow is a poor choice to emphasize a word because it is so hard to see the shadow in many cases.

All Caps used to be an acceptable way to emphasize a word. Today all capital words are shouting at the person and will not be viewed favorably.

Word Art is a feature that allows you to distort the letters of the font in a variety of ways. Unfortunately, many of these effects end up looking amateur and should be used with caution.

Highlighting is probably the most effective way to emphasize words and is done by placing a colored rectangle behind the text box which creates the same effect as a highlighter has on a printed page.

Coloring fonts in your presentation can be a useful information trigger for your audience. Pick your main color by finding the contrasting color to your background. Once you have set that color, pick a second color for your titles.

Finally, pick other colors as needed to indicate links, buttons, or special meanings. Once you pick your colors, stick to them consistently. Don't use green for button text in one part of a presentation and yellow in another. You will confuse your audience and make it harder for them to use your presentation.

The last topic that I will cover about fonts and text are bullet points. Using bullet points on a slide is a great way to present the key ideas during a presentation. When selecting a bullet to use, consider these ideas:

First, let's look at the bullet character. The most popular choices are a filled circle, filled square, open circle, hyphen, and arrow. The characters with a large portion of the character-filled are easier to see by the audience and are preferred. You can select a graphic as a bullet, but make sure that it does not detract from the slide by drawing too much attention away from the words on the slide. If you are using simple text and more graphics, bullets might not even be needed. Just make sure the bullet is adding clarity and organization to the presentation and not just another object on the screen.

Next, how about bullet size? As a rule, try to select a bullet size slightly smaller than the font of the text so it does not overpower the text itself.

Third, you want appropriate bullet spacing. Make sure that there is enough space between the bullet and the first letter of the text so that the first word is readable.

When you are finished selecting and tweaking your fonts and text go through your presentation to make sure all your text is legible. Have you kept the words on your slides to a minimum, letting them serve as cues for elaboration? Remember that the fastest way to lose your audience is to read slide text to them verbatim. Make sure you haven't crammed too much text on a slide. Also, check that you've used a large enough font in a readable color and there aren't any conflicting background colors or designs.

Images

Images are key elements of every presentation. Your audience has ears and eyes. They will want to see what you're talking about, and a good visual cue will help them to understand your message much better. Here are some general rules about using images in your presentations:

1. Have more images in your slides than text.
2. But do not use images to decorate!
3. Images can reinforce or complement your message.
4. Use images to visualize and explain.
5. A picture can say more than a thousand words.

Presentations with images tell the story with pictures. When you illustrate with images it makes it easier to explain difficult points and generate interest. Images allow you to simplify tough subjects using examples. When an audience member has a concept explained and can see a picture, the brain will attach that explanation to the visual queue. This increases the audience's interest and retention. Remember, a mental picture is worth a thousand words. You notice that I said a mental picture is worth a thousand words, not a picture. The mental picture is the image plus some explanation associated with it.

We should give up the false belief that any picture is worth a thousand words. We are so convinced that an image trumps words that we fool ourselves into believing that everyone will get what we mean, no matter what image we choose. Trust me, nobody gets what we mean until we tell them what we mean. The image just can't stand alone. There are three typical misconstructions I come across when it comes to presentation images.

First, images can mean different things to different people. If I show you an image by itself and ask what it means, I will probably get all kinds of answers. Even if I asked the meaning it might have in the context of presenting. Here is an image and here are some of the answers that I get:

1. Chaos
2. Structure
3. Bridge
4. It means nothing to me

The answers may vary depending on what we talked about before or what happened on the way to the office. So, don't assume that each member of your audience will take the same meaning from an image.

Secondly, images can evoke unexpected reactions. The person who used this image was talking about vegetables and was illustrating broccoli. The image started a discussion that the speaker hadn't expected:

The reactions from this picture were:

1. This is creepy.
2. It looks like an alien landscape

3. Cool... what is it?
4. It makes me feel uneasy.
5. Why didn't you just use a spear of broccoli?

Every image carries emotions. Make sure it carries the ones you want. Cold black-and-white-and-green colors won't help when you're after warm and friendly. I have seen some seriously offensive images in presentations. I often wonder what the author was thinking.

Lastly, what's clear to you may not be clear to your audience. If you need quite a few verbal explanations, then the image probably is not effective at representing your message. Sometimes you just must go with a tried-and-true image to get the job done. There's a disturbing trend that I have noticed recently. The use of irrelevant images in presentations. Stock photo sites have made it easy to find stunning images. The problem is the images often have nothing to do with the subject of the presentation. At best, the images become background wallpaper to the presentation. At worst the images are visually distracting. Here's a checklist of ways you might be misusing images in your presentation:

1. Teaming a random word with an image.

Pulling one word out of a sentence and teaming it with an image is only useful when that word is a key part of your presentation. Random words don't deserve that prominence.

2. Clever metaphors/references in your presentation

The search engines on online photo sites make it easy to find clever images to illustrate your metaphors. Your audience should be able to understand your metaphor or reference just by looking at the image. If not, it's just interesting wallpaper or worse – it will take the focus away from what you're saying as audience members try and discern the connection.

3. Image is just too stunning/interesting

Then there are images that are just too good. Even if they're related to your point; the quality of the image may distract from your presentation. Once again, the audience missed what the presenter said next. And there's the temptation with great images to reuse them.

Use images when they are relevant to the point. Avoid these traps. Use an image only when it helps make your point understandable or memorable.

Use high-quality graphics, including photographs. You can take your own high-quality photographs with your digital camera, purchase professional stock photographs, or use the plethora of high-quality images available online. Be cautious of copyright issues when using online content. Never simply stretch a small, low-resolution photo to make it fit your layout. Doing so will degrade the resolution even further.

Avoid using Slideshow clip art or other cartoonish line art. Again, if it is included in the software, your audience has seen it a million times before. It may have been interesting in 1993, but today the inclusion of such clip art often undermines the professionalism of the presenter. There are exceptions, of course, and not all clip art is dreadful, but use it carefully and judiciously.

I often use images of people in my slides, as photography of people tends to help the audience connect with the slide on a more emotional level. If the photographic image is secondary in importance, then I decrease the opacity and add a blur or motion filter in a graphics program. If the photographic image is the primary area, I want the audience to notice (such as a picture of a product), then the image can be more pronounced and littler (or no) text is needed. Stunning photography can be memorable, but your audience may not remember the point. By putting some words directly on the image, you ensure that the image is linked with your point in their memory.

Along with images animations, video, and audio can provide additional layers to a presentation if they are used correctly. In animations, there is a fine line between a comic or professional impression. However, animations can be rather powerful tools to visualize and explain complicated matters. A good animation can not only improve understanding but can also make the message stick with your audience.

1. Use animations and media sparingly.
2. Use animations to draw attention, for example to your Take Home Message.
3. Use animations to clarify a model or emphasize an effect.

Using video clips to show concrete examples promotes active cognitive processing, which is the natural way people learn. You can use video clips within the slideshow without ever leaving the application or turning on a VCR. Using a video clip will not only illustrate your point better, but it will also serve as a change of pace, thereby increasing the interest of your audience. My company incorporates video testimonials from customers about various topics. The video is like an instant case study but even more effective. Instead of reading a case study, the audience sees and hears the client telling them about their success.

You can use audio clips (such as interviews) as well. But avoid using the cheesy sound effects that are included in the slide show software (such as the sound of a horn or applause when transitioning slides). The use of superfluous sound effects attached to animations is a sure way to lose credibility with your audience.

Make sure that you test any transitions, animations, and sound effects to make sure they work the way you want? I have seen when presentations are transferred from device to device, sometimes the graphics, sounds, and videos do not transfer. Did you limit yourself to only the effects that make the information easier for your audience to grasp (as opposed to running amok with spins, fades, dissolves, and canned applause and drum rolls)?

Charts and Graphs

The presentation of data is tricky. A sea of numbers on a page may make sense to an accountant, but most people hate to crunch numbers. For a presentation that explains budgets or statistics, you need to transform those numbers into charts or graphs. In this section of the chapter, we will cover how to use charts and graphs to present data.

Data-driven charts allow the audience to perceive your message at a glance rather than puzzling over a list or table of data. Furthermore, it is easier (and more persuasive) for the audience to see trends and comparisons on a chart, rather than to calculate them from the raw data. There are great advantages to doing this. Talking about numbers can be insanely boring or confusing. A chart will let people understand the issue immediately. With your chart as support, you can then speak to your conclusions, insights, and recommendations and tie it into your message.

As with any presentation or document, you must first understand the message you wish to convey. After that, you can choose the right data set and chart. Finally, you must make your chart both visually compelling and quickly digestible for your audience.

In general, one of the biggest mistakes in creating graphics for a presentation or document is using the wrong visual for your message. This is especially true when presenting data. The wrong chart only serves to confuse the audience or reader.

Four types of a chart can cover most data visualization tasks: the pie, the vertical bar chart, the horizontal bar chart, and the line chart.

Numbers don't lie, but a bad chart decision makes it extremely difficult to understand what those numbers mean. Before you put together another slideshow presentation, make sure you pick the right type of chart to clearly communicate the information you want to share.

First, understand the message you are trying to present with your data. When you're putting together a chart, you're trying to show one of four things with the data you have: a relationship between data points, a comparison of data points, a composition of data, or a distribution of data.

A relationship tries to show a connection or correlation between two or more variables through the data presented, like the market cap of a stock over a period, versus the overall market trend. If your message is about a trend over time, the line chart not only shows the values but also gives a visual feel for the rates of change.

A comparison tries to set one set of variables apart from another, and display how those two variables interact, like the number of visitors to five competing web sites in a single month. If your message is about a comparison of values, the bar chart is the most appropriate chart. If you are comparing shares from different categories, then a stacked bar chart works better than multiple pie charts.

A composition tries to collect different types of information that make up a whole and display them together, like the search terms that those visitors used to land on your site, or how many of them came from links, search engines, or direct traffic. If your message is about a share or distribution of a total, a pie chart or relative value chart is appropriate. Limit the slices to 4-6 and contrast the most important slice either with color or by exploding the slice.

A distribution tries to lay out a collection of related or unrelated information simply to see how it correlates, if at all, and to understand if there's any interaction between the variables, like the number of bugs reported during each month of a beta. Again, if you have multiple categories, such as years or product lines, a grouped bar chart or a pairing of bar charts work best. To show values from discrete time frames, such as sales total per quarter, a vertical bar chart may work better than a line. Charts created for frequency distributions and correlations will use lines and vertical bar charts.

Once you understand what message you're trying to send with the data you have, it's time to select the best method for displaying that information. Different chart types cater best to different methods. For example, scatter plots are best used to show distributions, while line charts are better suited for relationships. Pie charts do well when you're trying to communicate a composition but make for poor comparisons or distributions.

Juice Analytics' Chart Chooser tool takes the process a step further: The tool automatically picks chart types for you based on your selections and offers Excel and PowerPoint templates to download that help showcase your data properly. Check it out at http://labs.juiceanalytics.com/chartchooser/.

You've got your message, your data, and the right chart type. But how do you make it persuasive and memorable?

First, make sure you don't do your data a disservice by forgetting some basic design tips. Don't clutter your chart with too many grid lines unless they're necessary, or at least make them subtle so they don't distract from the information you're trying to present.

Make sure your chart is centered on the data you want to present, your axes are clearly labeled, and your axes have units on them where necessary, so no one must guess or infer what you're trying to say. Remember, your goal is that anyone can pick up your chart, whether you're there to talk to it or not, and understand what information the data is trying to communicate.

Use equations sparingly. Always make the math simple. If necessary, slow down and talk to the audience through the math part. Always ask yourself, "How much detail do I need?" Presenters are usually guilty of including too much data in their onscreen charts. Always use the least amount of detail that will convey the information and support your message.

There's also a matter of perspective. Advertisers and marketers are quite aware of how the eyes trick the brain when it comes to numbers. "$7.00" looks bigger than "$7" which looks bigger than "7" -- and that's why many high-end restaurants omit the dollar sign and the decimal point with two zeros. They go with a plain old "7" to make the price look smaller. You can use the same techniques to visually influence your numbers.

Also, tell your audience what to infer in your presentation. Along with the graph, put a short statement of your conclusion. All your audience needs to do is read the inference and see the proof in the graph. In fact, if you give the audience the conclusion, often they won't even look at the graph.

Next, consider incorporating images into your charts. Image charts are not only eye-catching and memorable but also help your audience grasp quantities and relative values quickly.

When not using an image-based chart, you can still follow some guidelines to make sure the chart supports your message as strongly as possible. Use the color (or the absence of color) to compare, contrast, and highlight the part of the picture that aligns with your message. Only show what is needed to draw the viewer to your message.

When you're showing data in the form of a graph or chart the audience can often get lost as they try and make sense of the data at the same time as you're talking. A concise sentence explaining the meaning of the data will prevent that.

All these suggestions will get you started, but there are no hard and fast rules for how data should be presented, aside from that however it's presented, it should be clear, communicative, and speak for itself. If you find that you're restrained by common chart types, then branch out to more experimental techniques. There's no reason not to let your inner designer sit down with your inner statistician. Be creative and come up with some intelligent and informative methods to present information, and you won't have to fall back on pie charts and bar graphs to do it.

When you come to the end of your presentation, what comes next? If you click out of Slide Show View, your audience will get a behind-the-scenes peek at your work, and you probably want to avoid that. Instead, end your presentation with a slide that maintains the presentation's master slide details but displays a simple message such as Thank you for your support or thank you for coming. I have seen many presenters end with their take-home messages. Of course, the end slide doesn't have to display a message. A blank slide might be adequate. You might even consider combining two end slides. Display a short thank you, or otherwise appropriate message, and follow it with a blank slide. That way, if you click out of the message slide, you're still covered. One more option is to end with the presenter's contact information if appropriate.

Chapter 6: Practice for Presenting

"There is no such thing as luck. There is only adequate or inadequate preparation to cope with a statistical universe." Robert Heinlein

Although it has been repeated many times over your lifetime, it still rings true. In any skill that you choose to pursue, if you practice it enough, you will be nearly perfect at it. There's no way to get around it. It takes a lot of time and dedication to be a disciplined practitioner of anything. However, if you can sit down, focus and try your best, you will see clear results.

I think that anybody who has achieved high proficiency at a skill has an appreciation for the value of practicing. Unless you are naturally talented at something or get extremely lucky, odds are the only way to "sharpen your sword," so to speak, is through repetition. If you are learning to play a musical instrument, a lot of time needs to be spent practicing before you play at the recital. Even the most accomplished musicians still practice. In the NBA, I see the top players come out before a game and practice the basics like free throw shooting. One reason why these people reach the heights that they do, and one of the reasons they remain there, is practice.

This mindset also applies to presentations. For most people, presentations make them nervous, which is natural. However, you can significantly decrease your nervousness by taking certain steps, carefully preparing yourself for the event to come.

Presenting is a performing art, just like the musician or the athlete. Always be looking for ways to continue to learn and improve your presentation skills.

Everybody knows the phrase "Practice makes perfect." The phrase should say "Perfect practice makes perfect." When you practice, you must practice the right things. Practicing bad habits is not very productive. When you practice your presentation skills, create a real-world practice as you can.

I have heard people tell me "I just go over the presentation in my head." A certain amount of visualization is good but good enough. I guess if you were presenting "in your head" it would be fine. Aren't you presenting out loud? Then practice out loud.

When you learn a language, a lot of practice is speaking. Speaking the language gives you the sounds and pronunciations and associates those sounds to the muscles that make them. Speaking the language gives you the opportunity to add feeling and emotion and even gestures to help you retain the meaning of the word or phrase. It also adds feeling and sound as senses to help you retain what you have learned.

Practice really begins with your concept. When you begin writing your presentation, you are in the process of practicing it. You are familiarizing yourself with the content as you create and organize it. Think about your message and the one thing you want the audience to remember from each point and how to transition between points. I will often talk the points out loud as I am creating them to get a sense of how the points sound together.

When you prepare your presentation, practicing out loud fills similar functions. It allows you to hear how your words fit together when spoken. It allows you to adjust your cadence and pitch. You can add emphasis or emotion to certain parts of the speech. You really don't want the first time you present your topic out loud to be in front of your audience. Words and phrases fit together differently when written to be read or written to be heard. Discover awkward phrases and tongue-twisters that you did not notice when writing and editing. Speaking the words out loud exposes flaws that reading does not. I travel a lot, so much of my practice happens in hotel rooms. I am sure that my hotel neighbors think I am nuts because I was talking to myself all the time.

Don't only practice out loud but do your rehearsal standing up. You get a more realistic voice projection, and you can try your gestures and how you are going to move. Reading your speech at a desk (or from your computer screen) is not optimal unless you are preparing for a webcast. Try to duplicate the speech setting as much as you can.

If you can arrange it, rehearse in front of a crowd. Standing in front of a group of people, giving your speech and seeing their reactions is a great way to boost your confidence in your material and delivery. Whether it's a small group of your friends, co-workers, family or even a random group of strangers, the action of giving your presentation allows you to see reactions and get natural human feedback. This will calm your nerves and make you more comfortable with the entire experience. Many times, you'll find that your worst mistakes will surface on this first go-around, leaving you with plenty of time and feedback to correct mistakes and re-organize your thoughts. Practicing with an audience is better than practicing without one, even if it is not your target audience. Be careful about taking their advice, especially if the presentation is fast approaching. The risk is that you try to incorporate changes you're not comfortable with, whether it's in the actual script or in your presentation style, and you end up causing more damage than good. Use all that you learn to edit your speech and make it better.

Don't only practice out loud and standing up, but also practice with distractions. I could sit in the peace and quiet of my home office and practice with no distractions, but that is not going to do me as much good. You might need some quiet time to memorize things and get a feel for what you're doing. Distractions might be practicing with other sounds or people walking by my office door because it makes me feel more confident that I can pull it off. For one presentation, the discovery visit revealed that the conference space had a big bay window overlooking the ocean. I practiced with an ocean screen saver on my computer monitor, so I would not be staring out the window during the presentation. I just did a videotaped interview and there were big lights and cameras and a white reflective wall next to me. I was totally nervous. Next time I will practice my questions with some big lights.

After the rehearsal, actively solicit feedback. Make it clear that you want honest opinions about what could be improved. A dozen "Good speech!" comments may boost your ego, but it won't boost the quality of your speech. Is your humor drawing smiles and laughs or is it missing completely? Are you keeping the audience's attention throughout? Are you receiving positive feedback in the form of nodding heads and smiles, or is a blank stare the most common expression? To reap feedback that will improve your speech, ask open-ended questions like these:

1. What was your favorite element in the speech? Why?
2. What would you like to see improved?
3. How can I improve my speech for next time?

This is far better than asking yes/no questions such as "Did you like it?"

If I had the perfect practice scenario, I would prefer access to the presentation venue the day before my presentation. I would do a dress rehearsal, on the same stage, with the same equipment. I have been able to do this, many times for my larger presentations. It makes a huge difference to me to be able to go through it once in the same environment.

As you practice, it's very useful to stop immediately whenever you notice a mistake or an uncomfortable moment and jot down a few notes. In any practicing situation, don't hesitate to analyze and re-analyze your presentation as you go. After all, therefore you're practicing in the first place. You can write down things like cutting down on time on certain parts, making sure you enunciate tricky words or refining the structure of your talk. You'd be surprised by how many issues you can find when you take the time to look at yourself closely.

Don't get hung up on specific words. It's unlikely that missing or changing any one word will totally ruin your presentation, so don't worry about perfection. The only person that knows you messed up is you. If you have trouble with a word that does not flow off the tongue, change the word.

The goal of practice sessions is to get presenters totally comfortable with the content, the slides, and the timing. Then, when the presentation is performed, they can concentrate on connecting with the audience. I know that I am comfortable with a presentation when I can think of the next 1 or 2 sentences while speaking. So, I'm on sentence #5 but my mind is already bringing up sentence #6 and #7. I don't have to think too far ahead but just enough that the transition from sentence to sentence is ultra-smooth and simple. Each sentence triggers a reminder for the next one. Find your own comfort zone. All the advice in the world won't help if you can't get comfortable with your preparation, practice techniques and ultimately, the presentation itself. Do whatever makes you feel comfortable. The more comfortable you feel, the more confident you feel, and the better things will go.

Timing is crucial in presentations, so practice your timing. It takes practice to nail down a solid time, but the general rule of thumb is to keep it short, simple and to the point. Since your goal is to decrease time while maintaining quality, practice trimming your message to include the most important and relevant information without the fluff. Set up a goal of the amount of time that you think is appropriate for your audience, then refine your talk accordingly. It is important to know that you can talk and convey the ideas that you want in the allotted time. The more comfortable you are with your time, the more flexible you can be as you give your presentation. You can easily do this yourself, but it helps if someone else can time you. When rehearsing, if my entire presentation is to last for 30 minutes, the practice time should go no longer than 18 to 25 minutes, depending on the amount of interaction or questions you anticipate.

PowerPoint has a built-in rehearsal feature that will record the time you spend on each slide. Are you ready to fill time or cut to the chase if things run too short or too long? Insert planned pauses and insert delays when you expect laughter or some other audience response. This may feel funny, but an accurate timing estimate will tell you if you need to do more editing.

Once you get more experienced, you will learn how many words can fit in a 10-minute time slot. Until then, however, practicing the completed speech is the best way to know if you are under or over time. As you get more experienced, time the individual sections of the presentation. Knowing the time for individual segments gives you flexibility if you need to rearrange your presentation at the last minute.

I generally practice my presentations in sections. This helps break the work into smaller pieces and gives me more flexibility if something changes. I'll focus on one part, memorize the core elements, run through it till I'm comfortable and then move to the next piece. Then it's just a matter of stringing the pieces together, which is easier. I did a keynote address for a national trade show a few years ago. I had ninety minutes for my presentation, and I had practiced it and had the timing down. When I got to the venue, the coordinator told me that the presentation had been "adjusted." Instead of ninety minutes, I now only had an hour. Since I practiced and created my presentation in sections, I was able to adjust on the fly. I just left out some sections that were less important to my main message. I jotted down my new outline on a 3x5 card and gave my presentation.

According to the Segmentation Principle of multimedia learning theory, people comprehend better when information is presented in small chunks or segments. By getting out of the Slide view and into the Slide Sorter view, you can see how the logical flow of your presentation is progressing. In this view, you may decide to break up one slide into, say, two or three slides so that your presentation has a more natural and logical flow or process. You'll also be able to capture more of the feeling of your entire presentation from the point of view of your audience. You will be able to notice more extraneous pieces of visual data that can be removed to increase visual clarity and improve communication.

The easy way to prepare for efficient time scheduling is to prepare each main point to be delivered in ten-minute segments. Frequently checking in with the audience to determine if they understand really helps. The audience participation keeps them feeling involved and allows the presenter to know if the audience is following and feeling connected or lost in a fog of overwhelm or confusion. If you see a glazed look in the eyes of the audience, change the pace by doing an exercise, opening for a brief review and question session or give them a quick break.
Checking in with the audience frequently can keep the presentation on track.

If I stand up to give a presentation and say, "This normally takes ninety minutes, but I will try to fit it in the ten-minute time slot." How much do you think anyone will absorb, understand, or remember? Nothing, right? What I can do instead is take one important section and thoroughly cover it. I can indicate that there are also sections on the other important areas. I can offer to set individual appointments or take questions after the meeting on the other areas of expertise.

Frequent checks with the audience during the presentation, asking for feedback sheets after the presentation and doing thorough honest debriefs after the presentation improve the productivity of each subsequent presentation. The goal is to enhance the enjoyment of each presentation now and continue to improve the connection with the audience.

Recording Audio

Another great practice technique is to know how the audience will hear and see you. First, let's talk about the audio, record yourself. I use my phone for this, but you can use a small digital or tape recorder. Record practice session and review the audio for places to improve. Record your actual presentation to see how you sound under real pressure.

Audio recordings help you gauge many delivery qualities, including speaking pace, pitch, and pauses. You can assess which phrases sound "good", and which are awkward to listen to. Notice when you stumble and determine why. Was the stumble caused by not knowing the material, or was there a difficult combination of words? By hearing and seeing yourself, you can judge the inflection, speed, and enunciation of your voice. You always want to put yourself in your audience's position, seeing and hearing yourself as they would see you.

It's not so much about perfecting your orating skills, although that is important, as it is about showing your personality through your words. To come across original and confident, you want to show your true character and that you're comfortable in your speech.

Look for places in the recording where your voice does not sound as confident. Listen to disfluencies. A disfluency is an unwanted pause, elongated segments, fillers such as "uh" and "um," repeated words, and editing expressions such as "I mean," and "you know." If you hear yourself saying the disfluencies, you will be more aware of them, and practice will eliminate them from your speaking.

Everybody has their um's and oh's occasionally. My disfluency is saying "so" between phrases or sentences. Since I have heard myself saying it on recordings, I am now acutely aware of it. When I say "so" once, it is so pronounced in my head that I instantly correct it. I am sure the crowd would never pick up on it, but I sure notice it.

Ask for feedback from your team. I tell my sales team all the time to let me know if they hear me saying any disfluencies. Once I was listening to one of my sales team members present. He started saying "OK" and then "K" after almost every sentence. I was sitting up front at the presentation. I wrote a large block letter K on my legal pad and started making a big hash mark every time the presenter said it. My team member looked down and saw that I was keeping score and saw the K. He realized what he was doing and corrected his speaking pattern in the middle of his presentation. Most of the time all you need to correct the problem is to realize that you are doing it.

Most presenters use these disfluencies to fill up all the space in their speeches. So, in the space between words, they say their "um's" and "ah's". Don't be afraid of that silence. In your practice sessions consciously work on pronouncing one word to completion and then the starting to pronounce the next word. Your enunciation will improve. Audiences need the small silent pauses between words to comprehend the meaning and retain information. Filling in those small spaces with sounds that don't contribute, even distract, from that process does you and your presentation a disservice.

Another way to record your presentation is by using remote presentation services like Webex or Go To Meeting. These services allow you to record your presentation including the audio, slideshow, and screens if you are doing product presentations. You can review the presentations later for analysis. The recordings can be used later for training other staff or clients.

If you think recording audio or web presentations is revealing, try video. A video recording of yourself speaking is an incredibly powerful tool. All your habits, both good and bad, are captured. If you have not taken a video of yourself presenting, you need to do it at least once. It is enlightening to not only hear yourself on audio but see yourself as the audience sees you.

In addition to the audio assessments mentioned in the previous section, you can also learn a great deal about how you are as a presenter. What do you want to look for when reviewing yourself?

First, listen to your voice. Are you modulating? That is, are you alternating your pitch and rate of speech? Are you speaking in a dull monotone voice? Look for expressive speech. Some people speak faster or slower, or louder or softer when they are nervous. When you review the footage do you seem confident with what you are saying. Are you showing signs of nervousness in your voice? Gauge your energy level. Does delivering this speech fire you up? We will talk about voice in more detail in Chapter 9.

What about movement? Are you standing with a white-knuckled death grip on the podium? Are you swaying back and forth as you are speaking? Are you pacing across the stage? Are you fidgeting, or displaying any other distracting mannerisms?

Examine and practice your gestures. If you are giving a presentation with nothing in front of you (like a lectern or table) then you need to be aware of what you are doing with your hands and your feet. Think about our hand gestures and how they relate to what you are saying. If you plan to move around, pace in sync with your words. I have seen presenters who will use hand gestures and walk to places on stage as cues for their speaking topics. Are your gestures working or are they distracting? Are your gestures well synchronized with what you are saying? Are your gestures varied or repetitive and monotonous? Movements need to be natural, confident, and purposeful.

Next, are you making eye contact with the audience? Eye contact is difficult to assess if the recording was made without a full audience, but you should be able to tell at least if your eyes are up, or down at your toes. Are you always looking down at your notes? Are you smiling?

If you are using visual aids, are your transitions smooth? If you are using a prop, was it handled smoothly?

A good question to ask yourself is, "Would I be excited to sit through this?" If the answer is no, time to change the presentation.

Many presenters that participate in a video exercise will discover mannerisms that they were not even aware of. In the world of poker, card players have what are called "tells." A "tell" is any physical reaction, kind of behavior, or habit that gives (or tells) the other players information about your hand. If you learn the most common tells, you can not only watch your own behavior to make sure your body language isn't telling all your secrets but also watch for the habits and tics in the poker players you're at the table with. Presenters have "tells" like poker players. Do you make certain gestures when someone asks you a question that you are not comfortable with? When you are nervous, do you rub your hands or scratch your nose? Something that I caught myself doing was rolling my eyes. I was watching a video of one of my talks and an audience member asked a "stupid" question. I gave the audience member the same eye roll that my teenaged daughter gives me when I ask her to take out the garbage. I didn't even realize I had done it.

Even though you are working hard preparing all the various parts of the presentation, you also must prepare yourself. I don't know about you, but I have to do serious mental preparation before every presentation. When I first started out making presentations, I was scared to death. My heart would beat so fast, I would literally shake. I had cold, sweaty hands and a dry mouth. I was embarrassed to shake anyone's hand. Gratefully, that has worn off over the years. Now, the bigger the room, the better. Speaking has become much less stressful, but it still creates some anxiety. Here are a couple of tips that have helped me:

1. Get a good night's sleep the night before and an important speech or meeting. Try not to burn the midnight oil before a presentation.

2. Don't schedule anything before the meeting. I get very focused before I speak, and I literally can't think about anything else.

3. Watch your nutrition. Don't drink too much caffeine or eat too many high glycemic carbs. These can disturb blood chemistry and can make you feel light-headed or hyper. This is my weakest point. I love sodas and drinking them is the opposite of what you should do.

5. Drink lots of water. Stay hydrated. I travel for most of my presentations, so it is important to stay hydrated on the road.

6. Close my eyes and consciously relax all my major muscle groups.

7. Take control of the narrative in my head and think positive, empowering thoughts.

Many of my presentations are followed by questions and answers. Have you prepared for the Q&A? I do a decent job on my feet, but if the meeting is important, I like to write out every question and objection I can think of and then write an answer or a set of "talking points."

When I first started presenting in my current industry, I approached Q&A as preparation. I got lots of practice answering questions. Before the presentation, I spent a significant amount of time writing out every question and objection I could think of. I categorized them by topic and put them in folders on my laptop. Whenever I was asked a question, I would simply go to the appropriate folder and start reciting the relevant talking points and statistics. It looked like I had mastered the material, but it was really all about preparing the material and knowing how to get to it when I needed it. Eventually, the answers became second nature. I think I get up to speed more rapidly because of preparation.

Practicing a presentation is a personal process and one that a speaker must experiment with to find the process that works best for them. Find your speaking style. Over time and with enough practice you can learn to speak and present in any style. If you're in crunch mode and don't have enough time, just try and find your own speaking style. Find your groove. Some people are ultra-enthusiastic. Some are much calmer. I'm not a flashy guy, so for most of my presentations, I'm aiming for enthusiastic confidence.

All in all, it comes down to carefully observing yourself and constructively criticizing the elements of your speech. You've got to take the time to truly grade yourself before you can expect to deliver a solid presentation. The true masters of presentations, such as TED speakers, train themselves and prepare extensively in advance for their talks. If you want to truly engage your audience, be yourself, but most importantly be comfortable with yourself. It's all about blending your personality with your message and finding the happy medium between your goals and the outcome.

Chapter 7: Setup and Positioning

"I went to this restaurant last night that was set up like a big buffet in the shape of a Ouija board. You'd think about what kind of food you want, and the table would move across the floor to it."
Stephen Wright

My first rule of setup is common sense, but it amazes me how much it is not followed. Arrive early! Give yourself enough time to properly set up before the presentation. Know your process and equipment and how long it takes to get everything going. I have timed myself. Know how long it takes you to boot up your computer, launch your presentation software, or other applications, connect and log on to your remote server, connect to the internet, etc. I personally know it takes me about 16 minutes to get everything I need up and going. I usually arrive at a presentation at least 30 minutes early, which is acceptable in my industry. Some of my larger presentations, I arrive even earlier. This gives me plenty of time even with the occasional hiccup. I have had plenty of experiences where you arrive a bit late, and you must go through your setup routine with all the attendees staring at you. That makes the setup time drag on forever. And, of course, that is the time that something will go wrong.

Again, the initial discovery should answer questions about the meeting venue. Collect information about the venue such as its size and layout, and the facilities that will be available to you to enable you to adequately plan for your talk. A particularly large venue for a large crowd of people may preclude the use of some types of visual aids such as a whiteboard. It is likely that these will not be visible to people at the back of the room. The size and acoustics of the room may also be important, will you be able to readily project your voice to the back of the room or will you require a microphone? Also, if you are distributing handouts to the audience, how will this be managed?

What equipment do you carry that needs to be set up or unpacked to put together. Do you carry a whiteboard or projector or screen? Always practice with your equipment before you get on-site to do your presentation. Write notes, if necessary, to operate any gadgets. I remember several presentations where the salesperson forgot the projector. We had to run out and rent one. Then when we got back to the room, we had to figure out how to operate it in front of an auditorium full of people. Not a good start to your presentation and this impression does not instill confidence with your audience.

I don't like it when you show up for the presentation and everybody (the attendees) are already in the room. You end up setting up all your stuff in front of everyone. You feel all eyes on you as you unpack your cables etc. The usual setup time feels like an eternity. This is also the time when something inevitably goes wrong, and you must scramble to fix the problem in front of everyone. I like having that time, by myself or with the team, in the room to get everything set up and configured and take a breath before jumping into the presentation. For me, this is a Zen-type moment.

For those people who use an agenda (we will talk more about agendas in the handout chapter) the setup time can be built right in. Put the setup time as the first item with a start time and duration. This makes the setup time an official part of the presentation, so the attendees are expecting a specific time frame for setup.

There is a big difference in setting up on your home court versus a Visiting court. Setup at your home location or a location you have been before being much easier. You already know where everything is. Setup in your own office and location many times can be done the night before. If you are visiting a customer site or a neutral site, you need to determine what resources are available to you and who will be providing what. I make it a habit, of at all possible, to visit the location beforehand to get the lay of the land. Simple things like knowing where the power outlets are (or if there are power outlets) make a big difference in stress levels when setting up for your presentation.

In addition to setting up your software, equipment, peripherals, there are also different ways to set up the room. I have been known to rearrange tables or desks or podiums into the configuration that I want or what I think will be most effective to deliver the message of the presentation. Seating along with related physical arrangements creates the foundation for presentations. These are often called room setups, and they influence comfort, access, and safety for the attendees. Also, when selected appropriately, the room setup extends a presenter's influence in the room.

Novice presenters often ignore physical arrangements and take whatever room setup is immediately available. If you, as the presenter or organizer, arrive at the designated room and find a setup that does not support your needs, change it, or request that it be changed, immediately. Experienced presenters understand that a functional setup is essential and arranging for it is not difficult nor expensive. It is a matter of planning and knowing the options. Again, here is where that discovery visit is valuable. Knowing the room set up in advance gives much more opportunity to change it if needed.

Personnel at hotels and conference centers are knowledgeable and usually ask about the room setup requirements. Convention and visitor bureaus also can provide general information about aisle widths and square feet per person. My experience is that it is more difficult getting the arrangements you require when presenting to smaller organizations because the group might not have the resources to provide extensive arrangement services. However, with small groups, it is very often easy to change the setup yourself. I have no problem moving tables and chairs around to increase the effectiveness of my presentation.

I will review the different room setups and talk about the advantages and disadvantages of each. Seating setups fall into two broad categories. Large groups are generally over 40 attendees and small groups, which are usually under 40 people.

Large Group Setups

The Theater style is the most used, but not always the most appropriate, style of seating for large groups. Other options are Classroom and Chevron styles. Presentations accompanied by meals usually use Banquet style (large round tables). Banquets have drawbacks but audiences are accustomed to turning their chairs and heads to see the speaker, crowded tables and noise from the foodservice. Let's look at the setups individually.

Theater-style supports a more formal presentation style where speakers talk from the front of the room intending that it be absorbed individually and passively by members of the audience without any reinforcement activity such as practice sessions, role-playing, or brainstorming. If the presentation involves note-taking or reference to handout material, Classroom style is a better choice as it provides a writing surface.

Theater-style

Pros

Accommodates most people per area.

About 10-13 square feet per person.
Appropriate for lectures and keynotes.
Note-taking cumbersome for the audience unless theatre has desktops.

Cons
Elevation changes needed for large groups.
No writing surfaces.
Minimal group interaction.

Chevron style is an excellent choice for audience interactivity. It is very flexible, good for either large or small groups and fosters a sense of audience involvement as the audience can see others and get feedback from them. Chevron can be adapted into Cluster seating for group exercises by audience members turning their seats around to face the table behind. Both Classroom and Theater can be altered to a Modified Chevron by angling the outside sections.

Chevron style

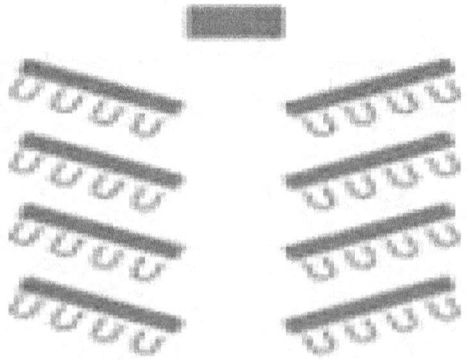

Pros
It provides a place for beverages and elbows.
Most interactive of large group setups.
Promotes a sense of participation.
About 20-23 square feet per person.
It can be set up with or without tables.

Cons

It creates a more enclosed feel for the presenter and audience.
More difficult to setup.

Classroom style is set up like rows of conference tables with chairs facing the front of a room (and usually a speaker), providing writing space for each person. This room set-up is ideal for notetaking, meetings requiring multiple handouts or reference materials, or other tools such as laptop computers. This is the most comfortable set-up for long sessions and allows refreshments to be placed within reach of each attendee.
Tables that extend beyond the stage or podium should be angled toward the speaker.
Allow for approximately 2' of space per person at each table. The minimum space between tables is 3'. Provide 3½' if space allows, for ease of movement in and out of rows.

Classroom style

Pros
The presenter can see all participants.
Accommodates large groups in less space.
Same as Theater Style but with tables.
About 17-20 square feet per person.
Supports notetaking and the use of handout materials.

Cons

133

Minimal interaction possible
Participants only see each other's backs.

Modified Chevron is a cross between the Classroom and Chevron Styles. This should be used when the audience in Classroom style rooms extend beyond the stage.

Modified Chevron Style

Pros
It can be set up with or without tables.
Improves visibility of speaker and visuals from side sections.
More interactive than Theater or Classroom.

Cons
More difficult to setup

Small Groups Setups

All the small group setups provide for and encourage the audience to take an active role in the presentation or meeting and to communicate with their peers. Small group room setups include Parallel, U-Shape, Semi-Circle, Hollow Square or Rectangle, Boardroom, Cluster, and Chevron.

Large group setups, such as Theater or Classroom, are sometimes used for small group presentations without realizing that they create a formal, impersonal atmosphere. This feeling may work against the learning goals and objectives of the presentation. A more formal atmosphere can present serious problems in learning environments requiring an audience-to-audience interaction like discussions, problem-solving, or honest feedback. When an audience can make eye contact with other members, as in Chevron style, the audience builds a sense of community and group learning occurs. Small group setups are ideal for planning or strategy meetings, focus groups, information sharing, status reports and introduction of new ideas.

A hollow square or rectangle is created with conference tables placed in a rectangular outline with an open space in the middle. Chairs are placed around the perimeter of the square. Small "brainstorming" sessions when the group does not have a designated presenter/leader. This provides plenty of workspace for each person and good communication and visual lines for each participant.

Hollow square or rectangle

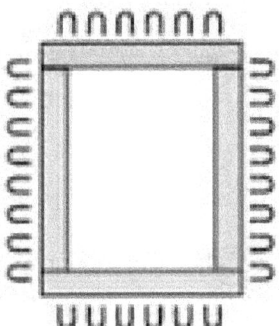

Pros
For meetings where hierarchy is not an issue.
Excellent for facilitator-led meetings.
Encourages audience participation.

Cons
Awkward to use any visuals.

The boardroom style is a rectangular or oval table set up with chairs around all sides and ends. This layout is often used for Board of Directors meetings, committee meetings, or discussion groups. Many facilities offer rooms with permanent conference tables in a variety of shapes. If these are not available, standard conference tables can be placed together to form a square, rectangle or hollow square. Remember, the larger the set-up, the harder it is for attendees to see others at the end opposite them.

Boardroom

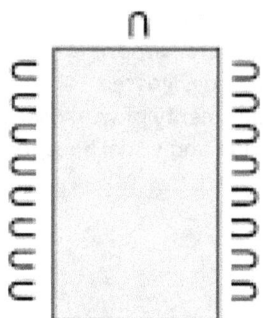

Pros
Very good for groups between 6 and 15.
Suggests formality and hierarchy.
Good workspace.
Good working atmosphere.
Good interaction between participants.

Cons
Not ideal for audio-visual presentations.
Not ideal for speakers.
Not ideal for larger groups.
Over 15, people at the far end table may feel left out and form a separate group.

Parallel Style is created by using tables or rows that are parallel to each other. This layout is often used for Board of Directors meetings, committee meetings, or discussion groups.

Parallel Style

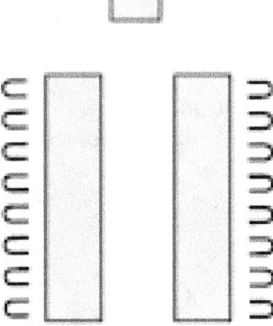

Pros
Seats can be on either outside or inside of tables.
An instructor can survey students' work.
An easy exchange between presenter and audience.
Center usable for exhibits or demos.

Cons
Not as comfortable if visuals are used upfront.

U-Shape is created using a series of conference tables set in the shape of the letter U, with chairs around the outside. This layout style is often used for Board of Directors meetings, committee meetings, or discussion groups where there is a speaker, audio-visual presentation or another focal point. Avoid the "U" set-up for groups greater than 25, as the sides of the "U" become too long and may not promote participation from all attendees.

U-Shape

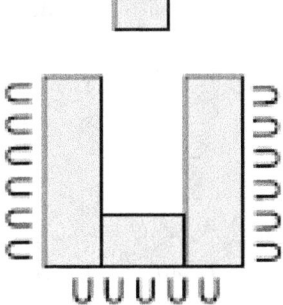

Pros
Good workspace.
Good interaction between participants.
Ideal when audio-visual or speakers are involved.
Encourages collaboration.
The center area usable for simulations and role-plays.

Cons
Not ideal for a larger group.

A Semi-Circle style is created by placing attendees in a half-circle configuration with the presenter front and center. This is usually a smaller more intimate setting for a presentation.

Semi-Circle

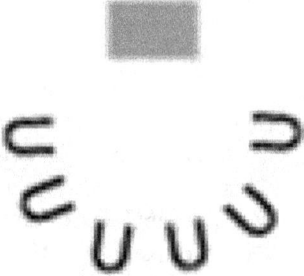

Pros
It can be set up with or without tables.
The presenter's role is minimal.
Excellent for sessions where sharing with other attendees is involved.
Encourages a sense of grouping and bonding.

Cons
Not ideal for a larger group

Cluster Style or Banquet style is normally round or square tables placed around the room with a view of the presenter. You see this configuration often in banquet halls where a meal accompanies the presentation. A variation on the Cluster or Banquet style is the Crescent or Half Moon, where the chairs are only placed on one side of the table for a better view of the presenter.

Cluster Style or Banquet

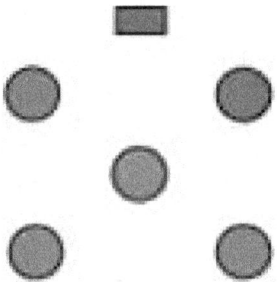

Crescent or Half Moon

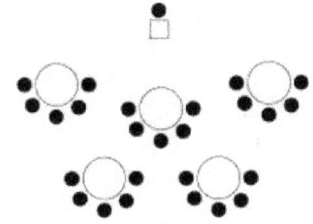

Pros
Good for presentations with breakout groups.
Clusters easily return to being a single group.
Quick and easy to follow with a meal.
Tables can be either round or small rectangles.

Cons
Not ideal for a larger group.
More difficult to control the room.

Don't compromise your presentation content and delivery with an inappropriate setup. One setup does not fit all.

"Where do you want me?" This is a question I have heard from many speakers and presenters. They arrive at the location to present and ask others where they should position themselves to do the presentation.

If you were able to visit the room during the discovery visit, you would have hopefully determined the speaking position. Sometimes it is not possible to visit the venue prior to the presentation. I have walked out on a stage before, looked around, and made an assessment. Do I walk across the stage to the podium? Do I position myself in the center of the stage?

There are better positions in the room from which to speak. One of the rules of a presentation is to increase audience attention and retention. The presenter wants to have the audience pay attention and remember what they say. You don't want the audience to fall asleep on you and not remember anything you said.

Should I stand up or sit down? Most of the time the best thing to do is to stand up. A presenter who is standing commands the room more effectively. Sitting creates a more casual discussion type of atmosphere. I do a lot of software demonstrations where I do a lot of work on my computer so sitting down is more effective in that situation.

Research says that the most effective place to be in the room to present is standing, in the front of the room, to the audiences left of whatever you are presenting. If you have a slideshow or materials being projected, or a flip chart or whiteboard, you want to be positioned to the audiences left of the visual. This technique works for audiences that read from left to right. If you are doing a presentation in a culture that reads from right to left, stand on the other side.

The audiences that naturally read from left to right, have natural eye movement in that direction, which means it is easier for the audience to process information that way. The presenter, being on the left, naturally draws the audience's attention. The audience listens and then their sight flows naturally to the right to look at the visually presented materials. If the presenter was on the opposite side, the audience's eyes go to the presenter, then must travel all the way over the presented materials to begin processing them in their natural order. The eye movement from the opposite side is twice as much work. This extra work increases eye strain and causes audience members to pay less attention and have less retention of the materials being presented. We have all seen audience members doing the head-bob because they are sleepy. Eye strain increases sleepiness for the attendees.

I performed a presentation in Oregon for a health center, and I had done several previous presentations with this group. When I arrived at the conference room, one of the attendees saw me and said, "There he is. I bet he wants his spot." He was sitting at the corner of the conference table, upfront, to the left of the screen. He remembered from the previous presentations that I had always located myself there.

Chapter 8: Speaking Voice

"It took me quite a long time to develop a voice, and now
that I have it, I am not going to be silent."
- Madeleine Albright

One of the most important components of public
speaking is the sound of your voice. It influences the impact
of your message and might even make or break the success
of your speech. Fortunately, for many people, good voice
quality can be learned. You must pay special attention to
your speaking voice if you want to communicate effectively
and positively influence your audience. From the moment
that you stand up to speak, your audience is judging you. As
soon as you open your mouth, if you mumble, or your voice is
too loud or too soft, your first impression will become
negative. Your voice is a speaker's greatest tool. When you
speak, your voice is the primary link between you and your
audience.

Your voice can reveal as much about your personal
history as your appearance. The sound of a voice and the
content of speech can provide clues to an individual's
emotional state and a dialect can indicate their geographic
roots. The voice is unique to the person to whom it belongs.
For instance, if self-esteem is low, it may be reflected by
hesitancy in the voice, a shy person may have a quiet voice,
but someone who is confident in him/herself will be more
likely to have command of their voice and clarity of speech.

Most presenters do not work on their voices and do
not maximize their potential. Most likely your optimum
speaking voice is hidden under layers of bad speech habits.
You must practice and perfect your voice, just like any skill. In
this chapter, we will look at techniques and suggestions to
improve your speaking voice.

Along with body language, when you talk, your voice
reflects your emotional state of mind. If the tones of your

voice are harsh or unfriendly, you cannot hope to persuade or influence others. A harsh tone is catastrophic in a sales presentation situation. A requirement for a good speaking voice is just the opposite of harsh. The quality of friendliness is what you are looking for, or I guess more to the point, listening for. The quality of your voice is largely a matter of habit, as is the unfriendly tone.

Another place to look from improved voice quality is attitude. Since the quality of your voice reflects your emotional state, if you are in a bad state, your voice quality is affected. If you are mad or frustrated, it is difficult to produce the genial, cheerful, and warm tones that characterize a good speaking voice. As a presenter, you may need to do more than simply develop your voice. You may have to reassess how you look at yourself, other people, and events in general.

A speaker should be to develop a voice that is:

1. Pleasant - giving a sense of warmth
2. Natural - reflecting your own personality
3. Sincere - needs to be believable
4. Dynamic - giving the impression of strength but no loud
5. Expressive - able to show various shades of meaning

First, let's look at what kind of voice you have. This will let you know what characteristics of your voice that you need to improve. Then we will discuss methods and techniques to make those improvements.

Do you have a loud or soft voice? Voice volume should ideally be appropriate in loudness and intensity. The level should vary to add emphasis or impact. Some people speak too loudly, and some people are at the other extreme and can barely be heard. Does your voice fade? Some people I know start off strong, but as they talk their voice gets quieter and quieter. If you want to communicate with your audience, you must learn to project your voice at appropriate levels.

Are You Monotone or Multi-Tone? Do your spoken sentences sound flat or do your voice tones vary. Good speakers vary their speech to express emotion and conviction. The highness or lowness in the sound of your voice is known as pitch. If your voice has an extreme pitch, then you should work on your pitch. Do people find your vocal range pleasant?

Do you mumble or articulate? The term articulation refers to how distinctly you formulate your words when you speak. It includes both how you pronounce individual words and how clearly you create speech sounds. Pronunciation is the formation and utterance of words. It is the product of correct sounds in the sequence of a word. Mispronunciation, on the other hand, is the failure to produce the correct sounds.
Enunciation relates to the fullness and clarity of speech sounds. Pronunciation and enunciation combine to form the basis of articulation or the shaping of sounds by the tongue, teeth, palate, lips, and nose. Clear articulation requires three conditions:

1. The sound must be accurately formed.
2. The sound must be sufficiently supported by the breath.
3. The sound must be finished.

Are you a slow talker or a fast talker? Your speech rate is closely associated with your personality. Your rate of speech is usually difficult to change because it relates to a variety of influences including experiences, family, thought processes, and culture. You should aim to speak at between 120 to 160 words per minute. Avoid speaking either too slow or too fast because can distort your voice quality. Slow speakers may not realize how listeners must struggle to pay attention to. People think at a much faster rate than the flow of speech, so overly slow speech encourages listeners to daydream. Talking too fast creates similar problems. When information is spewed forth at a rapid rate, listeners become frustrated and stop paying attention.

Now that we are familiar with some common differences in the types of speech issues, the next step is to analyze your voice. This will tell you what needs improvement. Use the speech profile at the end of this chapter to document your vocal characteristics and discover if there are any problem areas. Arrange to have someone that you trust document the characteristics of your voice. The items that receive lower scores are the topics that you need to work on and practice.

How to Improve Your Speaking Voice - Breathing

Now that you know your voice problems, the exercises in the rest of the chapter will show you how to improve your voice. Your goal should be maximum vocal output with minimum effort. An efficient voice is smooth, versatile, and produced with very little effort. For extreme cases, consult a speech therapist or vocal coach.

The first thing you can do to improve your voice is to improve your breathing. You need to breathe to talk and how you breathe impacts how you talk. Good breathing is essential for two reasons. First, by using full lung capacity the breath will support the voice and the voice will become richer, fuller and stronger. Second, breathing deeply and rhythmically has a calming and therapeutic effect as it releases tension and promotes relaxation.

Correct, natural breathing is the foundation of a good voice. Deep, controlled breathing is necessary for good vocal production. Your voice is supported by a column of air, the depth and steadiness of which determine your vocal quality.

By using full lung capacity, the breath will support the voice and the voice will become richer, fuller and stronger. This will benefit individuals who have a small voice and who worry that they cannot be heard when speaking to a group of people. Volume is controlled in the abdomen not in the throat, so breathing to full strength will allow for greater control of the voice.

Breathing deeply and rhythmically has a calming and therapeutic effect as it releases tension and promotes relaxation. Individuals who are relaxed are more balanced, receptive and confident. It is no coincidence that several religions use rhythmic breathing techniques such as meditation, yoga and silent contemplation, and vocal release in the form of chants, mantras or hymn singing as aids to their devotions. By easing physical tension, mental stress decreases and the mind is effectively freed to follow creative pursuits.

If you're like most people, you've been breathing wrong for most of your life. You would think something simple as breathing would be hard to mess up. Take a breath. Did your chest and shoulders rise? Yes? You just failed at breathing. When your chest and shoulders rise when you breathe, it means you're breathing with your chest. This sort of breath is weak and squeezes the throat area, causing strain on your voice. Proper breath originates in the diaphragm. You know you're breathing correctly if your belly moves in and out and your chest and shoulders stay still. Watch how a baby breathes. This is how they do it. For some reason, we pick up poor breathing habits as we get older and start breathing from our chests.

When you breathe in, your abdominal wall expands, and the dome-shaped diaphragm flattens. When you exhale, the diaphragm relaxes and the abdominal wall contracts. The relaxed diaphragm rises, pushing air out of the lungs. The exhaled air provides the controlled production of speech sounds. As the air pushes upward against the vocal cords, it causes them to momentarily separate, allowing the air to pass between them. The rush of air and the elasticity of the vocal cords then pulls them back together. The production of these vibrations is called phonation.

Breathing from your diaphragm when you speak does a few things for your voice. First, it gives your voice more power. Try it. Say a few lines of gibberish but focus on beginning your breath from your diaphragm. Imagine you're pushing your voice out from your belly and out your mask. The harder you push, the louder your voice will be. Speak as loudly as you can using this technique. Notice how your voice fills the room, yet there isn't any strain on your throat. Pretty cool, huh?

Breathing Exercise

Stand in an easy position with your feet one pace apart, with the knees 'unlocked' and not rigidly pushed back. Keep the spine straight, head balanced, and face muscles relaxed. Breathe into a slow count of three, then out to a slow count of three.
Try not to raise your shoulders as you breathe. Breathe in through your nose and out through your mouth. Consciously think of your breath 'filling down' to the bottom of your lungs. Put the palm of your hand flat against your abdomen and feel the movement. Push slightly against your hand as you breathe in and out.
Repeat this exercise ten times.

Depending on how you feel after several days of doing this exercise, extend the count of the out-going breath from three to four, five and six gradually building up to ten before you need to take another breath. Then count out loud on the out-going breath from one to ten. Repeat five times.

By building up your control of out-going breath, you will never sound 'breathy' or feel you are 'running out of breath' when you speak to a group or a meeting.

The second benefit of breathing from your diaphragm is that it does deepen your voice a bit without the ill-effects of trying to speak from your throat. Your voice will have more resonance and power as you breathe correctly.

Lastly, when under stress an individual's breathing pattern will change. When your muscles are tense you cannot use your lungs to their full capacity. When a person is frightened or nervous, a common symptom is tension in the neck and shoulders. This occurs because, when under pressure, over-breathing tends to occur. Plenty of air is inhaled, but with fast breathing, there is not enough time to exhale and relax.

How to Improve Your Speaking Voice - Natural Tone

Now that we have breathing down, let's get to work to develop your natural voice. Alright, so we all can't sound like James Earl Jones, but that doesn't mean we can't work on developing a more pleasant-sounding voice. I hear presenters all the time working very hard to talk in like a radio announcer. If it is not the presenter's natural voice, it comes off sounding artificial and staged. I've learned that we'd all be better served if we spent our time developing our natural voices to their full potential, not artificially lowering them.

If your voice is higher pitched than you'd like, despair not. Both Abraham Lincoln and Theodore Roosevelt had higher-pitched voices, and yet each was a memorable and convincing orator—because they made the best of their natural voices.

So, what does your best natural voice sound like? A good voice is one that is filled with warmth and expression. It should also have an even resonance that's easy on the ears. It should carry well so people can understand exactly what you're saying, and it should be flexible and have a wide range of natural pitches.

Unless you're a singer or actor, you probably haven't gotten any instruction on how to use your voice properly. Consequently, most of us have probably been using a sub-optimal voice because we've picked up voice habits that prevent us from sounding like our best selves.

To speak with your natural pitch and optimal tone, you need to project your voice from your "mask." Where's your mask? It's the area on your face that includes your lips and the bridge and sides of your nose. You know you're projecting from your mask when you feel the area slightly vibrate when you speak. When you can feel a vibration in that area, you know you're speaking with your optimal pitch and tone. A voice projected from the mask won't be nasal nor will it strain your throat.

According to a voice coach, Dr. Morton Cooper, here's how to focus in on your optimal pitch and tone that comes from speaking from your mask. Have someone ask you a question and answer it a spontaneous and sincere "mmm-hmmm." Keep your lips closed and let your inflection rise on the "hmmm." Pay attention to a slight vibration in your mask area.

"Mmm-hmmm."

Did you feel the vibration in your mask? That mmm-hmmm is your natural pitch and tone. Now say "mmm-hmm-one, mmm-hmmm-two, mmm-hmmm-three, etc." Check to see if the numbers are the same pitch and tone as your mmm-hmms. From here on out, focus on speaking with that optimal pitch and tone. It will take some practice, but it will be well worth the effort.

It is important to get used to the sound of your own voice. Most people are more relaxed in a private situation, particularly at home, where there are no pressures to conform to any other social rules and expectations. This is not the case in public situations when there are all sorts of influences exerted upon the way people speak.

Try recording your own voice in an informal setting, like at home. Listen carefully to how you sound in order to become accustomed to your own voice. You might also note any aspects of your speech which reduce the overall effectiveness of your message. Often people don't like the sound of their own recorded voice. This is the same way that some people don't like photographs of themselves. People can feel embarrassed about how they look and how they sound. Most of us are not used to hearing our own voices and these feelings are totally normal. Get past the initial, 'Do

I really sound like that?' stage and develop a better understanding of your voice.

When relaxed you will feel more confident, therefore by listening to your voice at home you will have an idea of how you sound to other people. Although you cannot hear your voice in the same way that others hear you, you can develop an awareness of its impact on others. Understanding the physical nature of your voice will give you more control over the way that you use it.

How to Improve Your Speaking Voice - Vocal Production

The following six core elements of vocal production need to be understood for anyone wishing to become an effective speaker:

Volume - to be heard.
Clarity   - to be understood.
Variety   - to add interest.
Pace   - to change rate.
Pitch   - to add emphasis.
Pause   - to add tension.

The first topic of vocal production is volume. This is not a question of treating the voice like the volume control on the TV remote. Some people have naturally soft voices and physically cannot bellow. Additionally, if the voice is raised too much, the tonal quality is lost. Instead of raising the voice it should be 'projected out'. Support the voice with lots of breath. The further you want to project the voice out, the more breath you need. When talking to a group or meeting, it is important to never aim your talk to the front row or just to the people nearest you but to consciously project what you have to say to those furthest away. By developing a strong voice, as opposed to a loud voice, you will be someone positive. By raising or lowering volume occasionally, you can create emphasis. If you drop your voice to almost a whisper (if it is projected) for a sentence or two, it will make your audience suddenly alert, be careful not to overuse this technique.

Second, some people tend to speak through clenched teeth and with little movement of their lips. It is this inability to open mouths and failure to make speech sounds with precision that is the root cause of inaudibility. The sound is locked into the mouth and not let out. To have good articulation it is important to unclench the jaw, open the mouth and give full benefit to each sound you make, paying attention to the ends of words. This will also help your audience as a certain amount of lip-reading will be possible. Simple techniques like this go a long way to improving the clarity of your speech.

Variety is the spice of life, and it certainly makes speeches more interesting as well. To make speech more effective and entertaining, certain techniques can be applied. Adding enthusiasm and emotional connections to your speaking will greatly increase the variety. You have huge potential available to you using your voice. Anything less runs the danger of leaving your audience bored, unimpressed, and missing the excitement your voice can add to your material. Your content gives listeners the information they need. Your voice makes that content come alive. However, it is important not to sound false or as if you are giving a performance. Whilst words convey meaning, how they are said reflects feelings and emotions. Vocal variety can be achieved by variations in pace, pitch, and pause.

Fourth, the pace is the speed at which you talk. If you speak too quickly, people can't keep up. If you speak too slowly, people will lose interest. Nevertheless, it is a good idea to vary the pace. Quickening up at times and then slowing down will help to maintain interest. Moderate your pace. This one is also closely related to breathing. Record your speech to determine if you need to change your pace. Get feedback from others.

The fifth is the pitch, which is the inflections or emphasis in your voice. When speaking in public, try to convey the information with as much vocal energy and enthusiasm as possible. This does not mean your voice has to swoop and dive all over the place in an uncontrolled manner. Try to make the talk interesting and remember that when you are nervous or even excited, vocal cords tense and shorten causing the voice to get higher. Emphasize certain words and phrases within the talk to convey their importance and help to add variety.

The last element is a pause. Pauses mean silence for a few seconds. Pauses are powerful. They can be used for effect to highlight the preceding statement or to gain attention before an important message. Listeners interpret meaning during pauses so have the courage to stay silent for up to five seconds. They are often referred to as dramatic pauses, and they convey authority and confidence. We will discuss pauses further when we talk about plotting your presentation in a later chapter.

How to Improve Your Speaking Voice - How to Stop Mumbling and Speak Clearly

Mumbling is when you speak and skimp on enunciation to the extent that people don't understand what you're saying. If you find that people often ask you to repeat yourself this may be a problem for you. I find if I must speak early in the morning, I have a problem with mumbling if I don't warm up my voice. I think that when my voice is not quite awake, I don't articulate my words well. To improve your articulation, the first thing you need to do is decide that you are going to be careful with your speech. You are going to be your best, no more careless, sloppy, talking. You can be aware of the mumbling habit and create actions to prevent it. Here are some techniques to try.

1. When you read, read aloud. Practice pronouncing words correctly and slowly. If you mumble, go back, and repeat the sentence. I used to practice this when I was reading to my kids. At the same time, I was teaching them to enunciate as well.

2. Stand up straight. Good posture will help to give the impression of confidence, and also helps to keep your airways open, so your breath can be stronger.

3. Slow down. Talking too fast is a common symptom of nervousness, but it won't help your words be understood. Many people who talk fast skip over sounds in words, which come across as mumbled speech.

4. Don't be afraid to say the wrong thing. Everyone makes mistakes and says the wrong thing occasionally. Just correct yourself, get over it and move on. Please realize that presenting is a skill and that it is something you can improve.

5. Open your mouth wider as you talk. When you talk closed-mouthed or with your teeth clenched, not as much sound will come out. Just opening your mouth, a little wider as you talk will produce more sound, which will improve mumbling.

6. Articulate. Make sure you stop the air for consonants like 't' and 'b'. Differentiate between your vowels. This is something that you will consciously practice and eventually, it will become natural.

7. Speak up. Try to speak at least a little bit louder than you do now. Speaking louder will require more breath so you will probably slow down and articulate better in the process.

8. Practice. Talk into a tape recorder or use your computer with a microphone. Then, listen to your recordings. Do take the opportunity to notice what is unintelligible, where your sentences trail off, and so on.

9. Listen to others who are good at speaking, such as radio and television announcers, and notice how they pronounce words, at what speed they talk, and so on. Don't try to imitate what they sound like, use them as examples of pace and enunciation.

10. Speak with inflection. Questions should go up in pitch at the end. Statements should go down. Notice, also, what syllables and words get emphasis. Try exaggerating your inflection, the way you would if you were reading to a small child and hamming it up a little bit.

11. Support from your diaphragm. Use the muscles in your stomach to support your breath as you speak. Even if you speak no more loudly, you will speak more clearly this way. Place a hand over your stomach, just below your ribs. You should feel the muscles there move as you speak.

12. Sing. You don't have to sing while anybody is listening but try singing alone in your shower or in your car. You'll exercise your voice and get used to using it. You'll also learn about using air, articulation, breath, and phrasing.

13. Shout. Don't scream or raise the pitch of your voice. Keep your voice at about its normal pitch and see how loud you can go. You probably want to do this alone or people will wonder about you. Cheering at a sporting event or talking over loud music is an opportunity to practice, or you could just close the door. Notice how you control your air when you shout.

Be confident. Have at least enough faith in the sentences you are saying to get them across clearly. Be conscious of your speech. Every now and then, listen to yourself and notice how you're doing. If you're nervous or uncertain, regard clear speech as a courtesy to your listener. Notice the words you struggle with, and repeat them loud and clearly, until you can say them at a normal speaking pace. Ask a friend to listen to you as you read a sentence. Then have them tell you what you need to work on.

How to Improve Your Speaking Voice - Voice Relaxation

Voice relaxation is essential for good speaking. As a presenter, you can't produce a pleasing tone when your throat muscles are tense or strained. Many people "talk from the throat," which means they hold their vocal tones too far back. This causes the throat and jaw muscles to tense, and the voice sounds harsh and squeezed. Throat tightness may be caused by nervousness, which is common for inexperienced public speakers.

A simple technique for relaxing your voice is called the Yawn technique. There are a plethora of voice relaxation tips and tricks that you can find with a bit of research. This seems to be one of the simplest and most common. You will start to notice a difference if you do these simple exercises several times daily for a few minutes each time.

1. Stand or sit comfortably. Place your hands lightly on your throat muscles. Speak in a normal tone. Note the tenseness of the throat muscles. Note the tightness of your jaw.

2. Yawn. Open your mouth wide. Finish the yawn with an easy "ho-hum," prolonging the "hum" for several seconds.

3. Drop your jaw as far as it will go without stress. Waggle the jaw from side to side and continue humming with your lips closed and jaw loose.

3. Repeat the yawning and humming. Notice how your throat muscles have relaxed. See how comfortable your throat feels with the strain removed.

Voice exercises should be done in brief segments, probably five minutes or less, and spaced throughout the day. If your voice tires or your throat feels scratchy, you are probably overdoing the exercises or doing them incorrectly. Before any relatively important speaking situation, it would be beneficial to have a voice warm-up. The voice is an instrument, and no musician arrives at a concert hall and launches into their set without first tuning up. The length of time and frequency of a warm-up is up to you and to a large extent depends on how much speaking you do or need to do.

How to Improve Your Speaking Voice -

An effective voice isn't necessary just for public speaking. A good, controlled voice is an asset in every contact with others. Your voice mirrors your personality with a language all its own. A natural voice that projects cordiality, cultivation, and authority is a significant tool for personal success. It can help in gaining promotions, making sales, winning the respect of others, and improving your social opportunities, as well as in speaking effectively to audiences. But most likely you can develop the sort of voice that wins favorable attention and reflects the qualities you wish to project. You simply must strip away any bad speech habits and replace them with positive ones that will enhance your speaking voice.

Here is a sample speech profile to use in assessing what aspects of your voice need improvement and what areas are correct. Have a coworker or friend that can give you honest feedback to perform the evaluation. You can give a speech to the evaluator or better yet, have the evaluator attend one of your presentations to evaluate your speaking under real-world conditions.

Negative	1	2	3	4	5	Positive
Variety:						
No Emotion						Full of Emotion
Unfriendly						Friendly
Stressed						Natural
Monotone						Multi-Tone
Articulation:						
Mispronunciation						Pronunciation
Mumbling						Clear
Tight mouth						Open mouth
Stutter						Controlled
Mushy						Crisp
Projection:						
Can't be heard						Easily heard
Flat tone						Dynamic tone
Quality:						
Nasal						Clear
Breathy						Clear

Harsh					Easy to listen to
Dull					Enthusiastic
Pitch:					
High					Low
Mono					Varied
Timing:					
Hesitant					Deliberate
Same					Varied
Slow					Fast
Jerky					Smooth
Nervousness:					
Jumpy					Calm

Conclusion

This concludes Objective 1 of Presentation Tactics, Strategies for Effective Sales Engagements.

We've explored the essential gear that can enhance your delivery, the importance of discovery in understanding your audience, and the valuable role coaches play in refining your skills. The step-by-step presentation prep, from building the content to utilizing slide show presentation software, ensures a seamless and engaging delivery.

Additionally, we delved into the significance of practice, emphasizing its role in boosting confidence and fine-tuning your performance. The importance of setup and positioning, often overlooked aspects, were thoroughly addressed to create an environment conducive to a successful presentation.

Lastly, we highlighted the significance of your speaking voice—your most powerful tool in connecting with your audience. By incorporating these tactics and insights, you are not just giving a presentation; you are creating an experience that captivates and resonates.

Please join me for Objective 2, The Mission, where we will discuss techniques deployed during the presentation. And Objective 3, After Action Review, to talk about activities after the presentation, like debriefing and evaluating feedback and techniques to help prepare for the next presentation.

So, go ahead, step onto the stage with confidence, armed with essential knowledge, and let "Presentation Tactics" be your trusted companion in your journey to becoming a masterful presenter. May your presentations be memorable, impactful, and leave a lasting impression on your audience. Happy presenting!

www.ingramcontent.com/pod-product-compliance
Lightning Source LLC
Chambersburg PA
CBHW071044290526
45795CB00004B/1308